The
Ada®
Primer

The
Ada®
Primer

An Introduction to the Ada Language System

Philip I. Johnson

McGraw-Hill Book Company

New York   St. Louis   San Francisco   Auckland   Bogotá
Hamburg   Johannesburg   London   Madrid   Mexico
Montreal   New Delhi   Panama   Paris   São Paulo
Singapore   Sydney   Tokyo   Toronto

Library of Congress Cataloging in Publication Data
Johnson, Philip I.
  The Ada® Primer.

  Includes index.
  1. Ada (Computer program language) I. Title.
QA76.73.A35J64 1985   001.64'24   84–21288
ISBN 0–07–032626–6

1234567890 DOC/DOC 8987654

ISBN   0-07-032626-6

The editors for this book were Stephen Guty and Jim Bessent,
the designer was Naomi Auerbach, and the production supervisor
was Sally Fliess. It was set in Century Schoolbook by The
Kingsport Press.

Printed and bound by R. R. Donnelley & Sons Company.

CONTENTS

Preface   vii

    Chapter 1 Introduction   1

Part 1 Fundamentals of the Ada Programming Language   7

    Chapter 2 Ada Language Basics   9
    Chapter 3 Data Description and Typing   16
    Chapter 4 Control Structures and Commands   23
    Chapter 5 Arrays   31
    Chapter 6 Subprograms   35
    Chapter 7 Tasks   40
    Chapter 8 Packages   48
    Chapter 9 Pragmas and Exceptions   55
    Chapter 10 Input-Output   61
    Chapter 11 Generics   74

Part 2 Ada Program Development and Management   79

    Chapter 12 How to Design, Construct, and Test Ada
                Programs   81
    Chapter 13 Management   107
    Chapter 14 Compilers and the Ada Programming
                Support Environment   124
    Chapter 15 Department of Defense Implementation
                of the Ada Language System   135

Appendix A Predefined Language Environment   140

Glossary   142

Index   145

Preface

What's in a Name?

Development of the Ada Programming Language is sponsored by the U.S. Department of Defense (DOD). The DOD named the language in honor of Aua Augusta Byron, the daughter of the English poet and writer Lord Byron; in married life, she was the Countess of Lovelace.

At Oxford University, the Countess became the principal aide of Charles Babbage, who in the early nineteenth century conceived the basics of modern computers. In her capacity as aide to Mr. Babbage, Lady Lovelace developed the principles of computer programming as we know them today. She is, in effect, the world's first programmer.

Ada is a registered trademark of the Department of Defense.

Philip I. Johnson

1

Introduction

1.0. What Is Ada?

The Ada Language System is the result of a U.S. Department of Defense initiative to establish and standardize a real-time, state-of-the-art, high-order language for modern "embedded" computers, i.e., computers that are integral components of larger systems.

Ada is one of the few major programming languages developed in the United States or Europe in over twenty years. It is the only major programming language developed primarily for modern embedded computer systems. These systems include microprocessors, and they frequently implement distributed processing, parallel processing, and additional sophisticated features not available when Cobol, Fortran, and other commonly used languages were developed about thirty years ago for first and second generation computers; machines now obsolete.

Ada is both a program design language and an application programming language. It includes facilities offered by common languages, such as PL/1 and Fortran, as well as operational features frequently found only in specialized languages, such as Tacpol, Jovial, and Pascal.

Ada is an evolutionary language. Therefore, it contributes to the computer sciences a number of unique developments that impact:

- System design and development
- Real-time concurrent programming
- Computer architecture
- Methodologies for test and validation

Unique Ada developments will be identified and discussed in subsequent chapters.

1.1. The Requirement for Ada

A Department of Defense (DOD) directive mandates that the Army, Navy, and Air Force begin using Ada in late 1983 and 1984. Other U.S. government agencies, such as NASA, are seriously considering Ada for major programming projects. In addition, Canada, most European governments, NATO, and the Common Market are implementing the Ada language.

1.2. Market for Ada

By requiring the use of Ada, the DOD in effect guarantees a multibillion dollar annual market for Ada programs. The DOD currently spends $5 to $6 billion per year on software for embedded computers.

1.3. Why Ada?

The driving force behind the defense initiative is economics. Testifying before the House Committee on Science and Technology on November 16, 1983, Dr. Edith W. Martin, Deputy Under Secretary of Defense for Research and Advanced Technology, stated, "The potential benefits due to the use of Ada have been estimated, via three independent studies, to be in excess of $1000 million per year."

As previously noted, the DOD now spends nearly $6 billion per year on computer software. Of that amount, less than 18 percent is spent on business applications, primarily written in Cobol. Most of the remaining 82 percent is spent for embedded computer applications for which a multitude of different languages are created and used. As the multibillion dollar figure shows, the cost of language proliferation is high. Ada will force the economics of standardization. Additional economics derive from the structure of Ada, the effect of which is to increase programmer productivity and to improve program reliability.

1.4. Impact of Ada

Inasmuch as the Department of Defense is requiring the Army, Navy, and Air Force to implement the use of Ada in the 1983–

1984 period, the effect on defense-related industries will be significant. In the near future, contractors will be forced to develop in-house Ada capabilities as a prerequisite for many new system developments.

The private sector needs Ada. Established programming languages such as Cobol, Fortran, and other specialized languages no longer fulfill the growing and complex present-day requirements of private industry. The result is that many versions of Cobol, Fortran, and other languages or subsets of languages are on the market. None fully meet the needs. Programming is labor intensive and very expensive. Programs written in Ada are cheaper to implement and support over the long run than are programs written in Fortran, Cobol or some other common language. Programmers with a good knowledge of Ada will be in demand.

1.5. Background

The Department of Defense initiated the Ada development in 1975 by establishing the Common High-Order Language Program. In July 1980 the DOD published a preliminary language definition from which a standard was finalized in February 1983.

The Ada design was jointly developed by the Department of Defense, major defense-related industries in the United States and Europe, and academic institutions in the United States and Europe. The NATO governments and their armed forces also provided input.

The Ada language development is not the first time the DOD has embarked on a computer language development program. The most popular general-purpose language now in use in both government and private industry is Cobol. This language was originally developed for first and second generation computers by the DOD nearly thirty years ago. What made Cobol widely used was not only its technical merit—outstanding for the period—but also the fact that DOD required Cobol on all defense contracts. This guaranteed a large market for Cobol and programmers trained in Cobol.

Then as now the impetus was primarily economic; the need was to replace a multitude of only moderately satisfactory early-day programming languages with a single superior language.

1.6. Who Owns Ada?

Ada is developed with public money. Therefore, the Ada programming language is public property, and the public is free to use it.

As noted in the preface, Ada is a registered trademark of the Department of Defense. The DOD will not permit anyone who develops an Ada compiler to use the name Ada until the compiler is validated by the DOD.

1.7. Status of Compilers

Programming languages require compilers. Ada compilers for a number of Army, Navy, and Air Force computers are under contract to private industry. In many cases, the host military computers and the target computers are the same computers that are used in private industry.

Efforts toward Ada compiler development are also underway in Europe. The European compilers are designed for European computers used by the NATO forces and private industry.

Compilers developed under U.S. Army contracts are not yet available but will be in early 1985. In addition, several companies and academic institutions in the United States and Europe are developing Ada compilers without government support. Some are already found on the commercial market. However, only a small number have been validated by the DOD. In this context, it should be noted that most early compilers are for a subset of Ada; they do not support the full language.

1.8. Operating Systems

For the past twenty to twenty-five years, computer manufacturers have provided operating systems with their computer hardware. The Ada programming language does not require a standard or full manufacturer's operating system. In lieu of an operating system such as that normally supplied, Ada requires (1) that manufacturers provide a minimal operating system and (2) that software support modules collectively called the Ada programming support environment (APSE) be provided. The APSE includes such software tools as linkers, editors, loaders, debuggers, and the like. The government may provide the APSE to computer manufacturers, system contractors, and other users of Ada as government furnished property (GFP). Also, the Department of Defense has issued contracts that include development of the APSE. Chapter 14 provides details on the Ada programming support environment. Information on the status of compiler and APSE development is provided in Chapter 15.

1.9. Implementation

As noted in Section 1.7 above, a number of Ada compilers are available in the commercial market. The Department of Defense recognizes this fact and has provided the following guidance to companies wishing to implement commercial versions of Ada in DOD Army systems:

> The Ada Language System (ALS) is the Army's Objective System. It will be used during the development and support phases of Battlefield Automated systems (BAS) developed under AR 1000-1 and the AR 70 series. . . . Until such time as ALS is available as a production system . . . commercially available, validated American National Standards Institute (ANSI) Ada systems may be used by BAS developers.[1]

The above directive permits the use of commercial Ada products in military systems but does not mandate their use.

1.10. Interface with Other Languages

The Ada language includes provisions for interoperating with program units written in other languages. Chapter 9 includes instructions for implementing such interoperation.

1.11. Ada Standards

The *Reference Manual for the Ada Programming Language,* published by the Department of Defense, was officially approved as the Ada standard by the American National Standards Institute (ANSI) in February 1983. The ANSI designation is ANSI/MIL-STD-1815A-1983. The DOD MIL-STD designation for the same document is ANSI/MIL-STD-1815A. The document may be obtained from the:

Superintendent of Documents
Government Printing Office
Washington, DC 20402

American National Standards Institute
1430 Broadway
New York, NY 10018

---

[1] U.S. Army Communications Research and Development Command Policy Statement 8-81, 20 March 1981.

1.12. What's in This Book?

As an introduction to the Ada programming language, this book is directed to programmers, engineers, business people, and students. It is not intended to be an in-depth analysis. Nevertheless, a basic knowledge of programming on the part of the reader is assumed. Chapters 2 through 11, comprising Part 1 of the book, cover the fundamentals of writing application programs in the Ada language.

Chapters 12 through 15 comprise Part 2. Chapter 12 presents Ada first as a system-program design language, then as an application programming language. Among major programming languages, the ability of Ada to function as both a design language and as an application language is unique. Chapter 12 also discusses linking Ada modules to form complete working programs, structured programming techniques, top-down design, abstraction and modularization, data hiding, and other programming methodologies. System test is analyzed in detail, and we also highlight the impact of Ada on computer architecture. How to manage system design, development, programming, and configuration control is the subject of Chapter 13. Personnel management is also discussed here. Chapter 14 considers compilers and the Ada programming support environment and, finally, Chapter 15 explains DOD implementation of the Ada Language System.

1.13. Department of Defense Management of Ada

The Department of Defense manages the Ada Language System from the:

Ada Joint Program Office
The Pentagon
Washington, DC 20301

Fundamentals of the Ada Programming Language

Chapters 2 through 11 cover the basics of the Ada programming language. These chapters introduce the technical fundamentals and the syntax of the language. On the basis of these chapters, the reader will be able to write application-oriented program modules in the Ada language.

The Ada Language System includes a number of unique contributions to the computer sciences. These features are noted and discussed in the contexts in which they arise at later points in this text. Readers wishing more in-depth material on the language are referred to the Reference Manual for the Ada Programming Language. *As previously noted, the American National Standards Institute designation for this publication is ANSI/MIL-STD-1815A-1983; the Department of Defense designation for the same document is ANSI/MIL-STD-1815A. The Ada primer is based on the January 1983 version of the reference manual.*

2

Ada Language Basics

2.0. Ada Language Structure

Ada is a strongly typed, block-structured language. It was designed
with three specific goals:

- Reliability and maintainability
- The recognition of programming as a human activity
- Efficiency

An Ada program comprises one or more separate and independent
program units that may be compiled separately, stored in a program
library, and later linked together. Program units may also be conceived of as independent program modules. There are three categories of program modules:

- Subprograms, defined as program units for expressing algorithms
- Tasks, defined as program units that provide for concurrent operations
- Packages, defined as collections of logically related program entities

2.0.1. The Subprogram

The subprogram is the basic Ada module for expressing an algorithm. There are two categories of subprograms, procedures and
functions. A procedure is a program entity comprising a series of

logically related statements. It performs an action. For example, it may read in data and modify or update variables. A function is similiar to a procedure but with one additional feature—the function returns a result. By contrast, a procedure cannot return a result. Subprograms are treated in more detail in Chapter 6.

2.0.2. The Task

In the Ada Language System, tasks are program entities that permit real-time concurrent, or parallel, operations between two or more program units. Multiple tasks executing concurrently may execute on multiprocessor systems, or they may interleave execution on a single computer. The task approach to real-time parallel operations as implemented by Ada is one of the language's unique contributions to the computer sciences. There is more on Tasks in Chapter 7.

2.0.3. The Package

The package is the Ada module for defining a collection of logically related program entities grouped or "packaged" together. A package may define a common pool of data or group together a collection of related subprograms, tasks, or a set of associated operations. In practice, Ada packages are collections of program modules designed to do common operations, e.g., payroll, file manipulation, etc.

The inner operations of the package are invisible to other program entities. Such units are allowed access only to the interface portions defined by the package specification. In other words, packages resemble black boxes, the interiors of which are hidden. Like tasks, packages are another unique Ada contribution to the computer sciences. They are explained in greater detail in Chapter 8.

2.1. Program Construction

As previously noted, Ada program modules are individual subprograms, tasks, and or packages independently written, tested, compiled, and stored in program libraries. Modules are later linked together to form complete programs. Two sections comprise an Ada module:

- A specification part which defines the program entities used in the program unit

- An action part—also known as the body—that comprises the sequence of statements that perform the functions of the program module

Frequently it is convenient to think of Ada modules as hypothetical black boxes. Such instances will be noted as they arise.

2.1.1. Specification Part

The specification part is that section of the program unit that interfaces with other program units. It defines the external characteristics of the unit. The specification also introduces the names and parameters of tasks, subprograms, and packages used in the program unit.

2.1.2. The Action Part

The action part of an Ada program module implements the series of operations that the unit performs. In common with other languages, the program statements are executed in sequence unless a control command or an exception forces execution to continue from another place. Generally speaking, the action section is not immediately accessible to other program units except according to well-defined rules.

2.2. The Ada Character Set

The Ada character set is similar to that of other high-level languages. As now designed, the character set comprises:

- The 26 letters of the English alphabet, uppercase and lowercase
- Numeric characters
- Common punctuation marks
- Arithmetic symbols
- Comparison and relational operators

The Ada character set utilizes the ASCII code.

2.3. Basic Ada Construct

The assignment statement is the basic construct of the Ada language. Its form as defined in the *Ada Reference Manual* is:

variable := expression;	(1)
A := B+C;	(2)

Line (1) is the generic format. Line (2) is an example assignment statement implementing the format. Letters A, B, and C are identifiers. As defined by the *Ada Reference Manual,* an *identifier* is the name of an entity. As line (1) shows, letter A is also called a *variable.* Identifiers and variables may be written in uppercase or lowercase in actual programs. To facilitate reading, this book uses only uppercase letters.

Identifiers and variables need not be only one character long as shown in line (2). They may be any reasonable length, but they must start with an alpha character. They may contain letters, digits, and the underscore symbol. Blanks are not permitted; therefore, identifiers two or more words long are written in this manner: MONTH_NAME. The underscore symbol fills in the space. An identifier cannot contain two adjacent underscore symbols.

The meaning of assignment statement (2) is that the sum of the values of the two identifiers, B and C, is assigned to variable A. Any previous value assigned to A is wiped out. The form of the assignment statement as described here is typical of high-level languages. The line numbers (1) and (2) have nothing to do with Ada; the line numbering is this book's technique for referencing program lines.

2.4. Reserved Words

There are about sixty-five reserved words in the Ada language. Declared identifiers may not use reserved words. The reserved words are:

abort	asset	delay	entry	if
abs	at	delta	exception	in
accept	begin	digits	exit	is
access	body	do	for	limited
all	case	else	function	loop
and	constant	elsif	generic	mod
array	declare	end	goto	new

not	package	record	select	type
null	pragma	rem	separate	use
of	private	renames	subtype	when
or	procedure	restricted	task	while
others	raise	return	terminate	with
out	range	reverse	then	xor

The reader may question the spelling of the reserved words **abs,
elsif, goto, mod, rem,** and **xor.** They are the only words in the
list that are not correctly spelled English. However, they are written
as used in Ada; therefore, the spelling is correct. The use of specific
reserved words will be explained as the need arises in subsequent
chapters.

In keeping with the practice of many writers, reserved words
will be boldfaced when used in program examples in this book.
Nevertheless, it should be noted that reserved words, when used
in actual programs, are not boldfaced, underlined, or marked in
any way. They may be written in either uppercase or lowercase.
The commonly accepted convention is lowercase; this facilitates programmer reading.

2.5. Documenting Programmer Remarks

Programmer remarks, or comments, are written following two hyphens for example:

$$A := B+C; \quad -- \quad \text{This is an example assignment statement.} \quad (3)$$

2.6. Mathematical Statements

In the Ada language mathematical statements are written in the
same format used in other programming languages. Examples are:

Addition: $X := A+B$ (4)

Subtraction: $X := A-B$ (5)

Multiplication: $X := A*B$ (6)

Division: $X := A/B$ (7)

Exponentiation: $X := A**3$ (8)

In common with other programming languages, the asterisk is used for a multiplication sign, two asterisks designate exponents, and the slash indicates division. Lines (4) and (5) are self-explanatory.

2.7. Order of Operations

The order of Ada operations is identical to that of algebra, i.e., the assignment statement is scanned from left to right. Exponential operations are performed first, followed by multiplication, then division, and last, addition or subtraction. Parentheses are used to group operations and establish priorities. Expressions enclosed by parentheses are evaluated first.

2.8. Exceptional Operational Situations

Execution of a program unit may lead to unexpected situations in which normal operation cannot continue. For example, an arithmetic computation may exceed the maximum allowed value of a number, or an attempt may be made to access an array component by using an incorrect index value. To deal with such operational problems, Ada provides for the use of unique program segments that will automatically handle the situation. Operational problems, such as the foregoing, are called *exceptions*. Chapter 9 contains explanations of techniques for handling exceptional operating situations.

2.9. Formats for Example Program Segments

Many examples of Ada programming are given in subsequent chapters. Inasmuch as these are actual program segments, they are presented in structured programming format.

2.10. Additional Ada Basics

In working with the Ada Language System, it is convenient to keep in mind the concept that declarations are elaborated, statements are executed, and expressions are evaluated.

Commonly used facilities such as input-output are predefined in the Ada language by means of predefined library packages filed in a program library. Such predefined entities are generic modules.

When wishing to use a library generic, the programmer calls it from the library, assigns actual parameters to the module, then uses it in a specific application. Generics are treated in Chapter 11.

Unique features such as the above and other additional Ada basics will be presented and analyzed at logical points in subsequent chapters.

Chapter

3

Data Description
and Typing

3.0. The Players Are Typecast

Computers perform some form of computation, either straight mathematics or alphanumeric operations. The elements on which operations are performed are called *data*. As previously noted in Section 2.3 and in common with other languages, data elements are called identifiers or variables. Identifiers may be as short as one ASCII character—eight bits.

On the hardware level within the computer, identifiers are collections of bits. Inasmuch as a collection of bits may have several meanings, depending on the context in which it is used, most programming languages provide a standard way of indicating the meaning.

In the Ada language, defining the meaning of an identifier is called *typing*. In other words, typing describes the attributes of an identifier. The process of typing specifies (1) a set of values for each identifier and (2) a set of applicable operations. Every identifier in an Ada program unit is defined, or typed. It can be used only in the manner permitted by the typing. To put it another way, Ada identifiers are like actors who can play only one role because they are typecast.

When programs are compiled, the compiler checks to see that all identifiers are typed, and further, that only legal operations—operations that are consistent with the assigned typing—are programmed. If the identifier is not correctly typed and operations are not legal, the compiler automatically rejects that segment of the program. It is on this basis that Ada is said to be a *strongly typed* language.

3.1. Ada Language Types

Ada types divide into four principal categories: scalar, composite, access, and private.

3.1.1. Scalar Types

Scalar types subdivide further into enumerated, numeric, and boolean types.

3.1.1.1. Enumeration.   Programmers define ordered sets in which possible values are explicitly listed. For example:

type MONTH_NAME **is** (Jan, Feb, Mar, Apr, May, Jun,
Jul, Aug, Sep, Oct, Nov, Dec);   (9)

In this example line (9) defines MONTH_NAME as a type having twelve values, the twelve months of the year. Each month is an identifier. The names must be spelled as shown above. No other name will be accepted by the compiler. Also in line (9), the boldfaced words **type** and **is** are reserved words. In this format, the two reserved words tell the compiler that line (9) is an enumeration type statement that lists as attributes the twelve months of the year.

A second example of the enumeration type statement is:

type SWITCH_STATUS **is** (OFF,ON);   (10)

Line (10) defines the status of a switch as either off or on.

A particularly important enumeration category is the predefined identifier CHARACTER. The predefined values of CHARACTER are the 128 characters of the ASCII code. (For an explanation of the term predefined, see Section 3.3.) An example type statement would be:

type CHARACTER **is** ('A', 'B'. . . , 'Z');   (11)

The technique for typing characters shown in line (11) may be used for other operations in addition to writing the textual characters of the ASCII code. For example, by using proper typing, we can use the same ASCII characters for an entirely different purpose, as line (12) illustrates.

type ROMAN_DIGITS **is** ('I','V','X','L','C','D','M');   (12)

Line (12) defines Roman numbers. Note that in both lines (11) and (12) the literals are written within single quotes. In line (11), the predefined identifier CHARACTER is typed with the twenty-six letters of the English alphabet. Line (12) types seven letters of the same English alphabet as ROMAN_DIGITS. Obviously, if lines (11) and (12) are both used in the same program unit, confusion will result. This situation is called *overloading;* it may occur in subprograms. Overloading is discussed in detail in Chapter 6, "Subprograms."

To sum up, in the above examples, including lines (9), (10), (11), and (12), we explicitly enumerated a class of values for each identifier. The enumerated values are ordered, i.e., they are listed in ascending value. Thus in line (9), for example, Feb is greater than Jan; Mar is greater than Feb; and so on. The largest value in line (9) is Dec.

3.1.1.2. Numeric.   The numeric type statement includes integer, fixed-point, or floating-point numbers. Examples are:

type PAGE_NUM **is range** 1 . . 200;   (13)

Line (13) defines a range of integer page numbers for the identifier PAGE_NUM.

type VOLTAGE **is delta** 0.001 **range** 0.00 . . 10.00;   (14)

Line (14) defines voltage range to an accuracy of 1 millivolt over the range 0.00 . . 10.00 for the identifier VOLTAGE.

type MASS **is digits** 7 **ranges** 0.0 . . 1.0E10;   (15)

Line (15) defines a floating-point representation to a precision of seven significant figures.

3.1.1.3. Boolean.   Logic types are scalar. The format is:

type BOOLEAN **is** (FALSE, TRUE);   (16)

Boolean types are predefined in Ada, i.e., they are written into the language. See Section 3.3 for an explanation of the term predefined.

3.1.2. Object Declarations

By definition, a *data object* is a variable or constant. It can denote any kind of data element. This means that we may declare objects of types already specified and use the values enumerated in that specification. In effect, this is an elaboration of the type statement. Objects are declared in this manner:

MONTH : MONTH_NAME;   (17)

Line (17) creates a variable called an object and named MONTH. It declares that MONTH is of the same type as the identifier MONTH_NAME. For line (17) to be valid, MONTH_NAME must be previously typed. In our example, this was done in line (9).

Another example declaration is:

COUNTER : INTEGER;   (18)

Line (18) creates a variable COUNTER of type INTEGER. The counter uses integer numbers starting with one. INTEGER is predefined. Object declarations such as lines (17) and (18) may be placed in either the specification section of a program module or in the body of that entity.

3.1.3. Composite Types

Composite types provide the means of defining structured objects formed from related components. Examples include arrays and records.

3.1.3.1. Arrays. Arrays have indexed components of the same type.

type A **is array** (1 . . 10) **of** REAL;   (19)

Line (19) defines array A as comprising 10 elements, each a real number. Note that in the array all elements are of the same type. The identifier REAL is user-defined. Line (19) is an example of a *constrained* array definition.

Line (20) is an example of an *unconstrained* array.

type VECTOR **is array** (INTEGER **range** ◇) **of** REAL; (20)

Again, REAL is user-defined. The symbol ◇ means an indefinite range.

3.1.3.2. Records. Groups of related items are frequently called *records*. Records differ from arrays in that components of a record may be of different types. The following example illustrates.

```
type MONTH_NAME is (Jan, Feb, Mar, Apr, May, Jun,
                    Jul, Aug, Sep, Oct, Nov, Dec,);    (21)
    type DATE is                                       (22)
      record                                           (23)
        DAY   : INTEGER range 1 . . 31;                (24)
        MONTH : MONTH_NAME;                            (25)
        YEAR  : INTEGER range 0 . . 4000;              (26)
      end record;                                      (27)
```

Line (21) types the identifier MONTH_NAME as any of the twelve months of the year. Lines (22) through (27) type the identifier DATE as a record comprising three declarative components: DAY, MONTH, and YEAR. Lines (24), (25), and (26) are declarative statements.

The three variables, DAY, MONTH, and YEAR, are object declarations, declared in the manner shown in lines (17) and (18). DAY is declared to be an integer number in the range of 1 to 31. MONTH is declared as a name. YEAR is declared as an integer of range 0 to 4000.

3.1.4. Access Types

In many programs we create dynamic entities during program execution. These units continuously change their relationship to other program entities. Typical examples are the varying components of a data base. We declare dynamic entities with access types.

3.1.5. Private Types

A private type declaration is only allowed as a declarative item in the visible part of a package or as the generic parameter declaration for a generic formal type in a generic formal part.

A private type defines within a package an operational structure, the details of which are not available to other program entities that may use the package. To other program entities, the package is known only by its interface specification and the set of operations defined for it. A private type and its applicable operations are defined in the specification part of the package. How to define and use the private type is explained in Chapter 8, "Packages."

3.2. Special Comments on Typing

In the opening paragraph of this chapter, we noted that typing defines a set of values for each identifier and, additionally, the set of operations in which the defined identifiers may participate. To make the aforesaid meaningful in terms of practical operations, consider the following example. As shown in line (9), we define—type—MONTH_NAME as:

> **type** MONTH_NAME **is** (Jan, Feb, Mar, Apr, May, Jun,
> Jul, Aug, Sep, Oct, Nov, Dec,);   (28)

On line (17), we declare MONTH as:

> MONTH : MONTH_NAME;   (29)

Recognizing the constraints outlined in this chapter, it is now evident that we cannot write the assignment statement:

> MONTH := MONDAY;   (30)

Monday is a day of the week. It is not a month of the year as defined in line (9). Line (30) will be rejected by the compiler. However, we can write:

> MONTH := Jul;   (31)

Line (31) will be accepted by the compiler because Jul is typed as a month of the year in line (9).

Two important rules, both enforced by the compiler, are derived from these examples:

- An identifier or variable can only be assigned values of its own type; it cannot be assigned values of a different type.
- The only operations allowed on identifiers are those associated with its type.

3.3. Predefined Types

We have previously said that the enumeration types BOOLEAN and CHARACTER are predefined in the language. The numeric type INTEGER is also predefined. The expression *predefined* means defined in an existing library package supplied with the compiler as a component of the Ada Language System. In addition to the predefined types already noted, there are a number of other predefined components in the language. These will be noted as they occur. A list of predefined types supplied with the language is given in Appendix A. Details on predefined attributes are presented in the annexes to the reference manual on the Ada language, ANSI/MIL-STD-1815A.

3.4. Strong Typing, Summary Considerations

In the introductory sections of this chapter, we noted that Ada is said to be a strongly typed language. Strong typing means that every identifier and every variable must be typed, or defined. Strong typing is a very important feature: It eliminates a major source of programmer errors since identifiers that are not correctly typed are caught at compilation time.

4

Control Structures and Commands

4.0. Control Structures

All computer programs contain structures that control the order of program execution. In Ada programs, control structures are placed in the action part, or body, of the program unit. In format, they are similar to control statements in other high-order languages. Two fundamental and important structural categories are conditional structures and loop structures. Conditional statements provide a boolean test, the results of which specify a course of action.

4.1. Conditional Control Structures

Conditional control structures subdivide into (1) **if** control and (2) **case** control.

4.1.1. If Control Structures

Ada provides a number of **if** control statements. Following is the generalized **if** structure from which all **if** control forms are developed.

if condition **then**	(32)
sequence of statements;	(33)
elsif condition **then**	(34)
sequence of statements;	(35)

```
    elsif condition then                             (36)
        sequence of statements;                      (37)
    else                                             (38)
        sequence of statements;                      (39)
    end if;                                          (40)
```

For the execution of an **if** statement, the condition specified after the **if** and any conditions specified after **elsif** are evaluated in succession until one evaluates as true; then the corresponding sequence of statements is executed. Any number of **elsif** conditions may be tested. The last test in the sequence is an **else** condition. For the sequence of statements following the **else**—line (38) in the example—to be executed, the **else** condition must evaluate as true.

If action is needed when no condition is true, write **else** after the last **elsif**; then write the necessary series of statements. If no action is required, terminate the **if** statement with a **null** following the last **else** and then write an **end if** on the next line, as in line (40) above. The following is an example.

```
    if TODAY is MONDAY . . FRIDAY then               (41)
        DAILY_PROCESS;                               (42)
    elsif TODAY = SATURDAY then                      (43)
        SAT_PROCESS;                                 (44)
    elsif TODAY = SUNDAY then                        (45)
        SUN_PROCESS;                                 (46)
    else                                             (47)
        null;                                        (48)
    end if;                                          (49)
```

The **if** structure need not be as complex as the above example. The following is a simple **if**. Given the problem: Double X if X is less than Y, and if X is not less than Y, leave X unchanged, in Ada we would write:

```
    if X < Y then                                    (50)
        X := 2*X;                                    (51)
    end if;                                          (52)
```

The above program segment says: If X is less than Y, then do line (51); if X is equal to or greater than Y, skip line (51) and jump to line (52).

4.1.2. Case Control Structure

The **case** statement selects for execution one of a series of alternative sequences of statements, the selection depending on the value
of an expression. The generalized **case** structure from which all
case forms are developed is:

case expression **is**	(53)
when choice => sequence of statements;	(54)
end case;	(55)

Any number of **when** choices—line (54)—may be used.

An example of how to implement the **case** structure in an account-
ing problem follows:

case TODAY **is**	(56)
when MONDAY => COMPUTE_INITIAL_BALANCE;	(57)
when FRIDAY => COMPUTE_CLOSING_BALANCE;	(58)
when TUESDAY . . THURSDAY =>	
GENERATE_REPORT(TODAY);	(59)
when SATURDAY . . SUNDAY => **null;**	(60)
end case;	(61)

The meaning of this segment is self-explanatory.

Shown below is another form of the **case** construct that is of
interest.

case BIN_NUMBER(COUNT) **is**	(62)
when 1 => UPDATE_BIN(1);	(63)
when 2 => UPDATE_BIN(2);	(64)
when 3|4 =>	(65)
EMPTY_BIN(1);	(66)
EMPTY_BIN(2);	(67)
when others => **raise** ERROR;	(68)
end case;	(69)

The example is a segment of an inventory control program. It
says that when condition 1 occurs, we execute UPDATE_BIN(1);
when condition 2 occurs, we execute UPDATE_BIN(2); when either conditions 3 or 4 occur, we execute EMPTY_BIN(1) and
EMPTY_BIN(2). Note that in line (65) there is an alternative choice.
When either of the alternatives occurs, the statements on lines
(66) and (67) are executed. In line (68) two reserved words, **others**
and **raise**, are used. **Others** is given as the choice for all situations

not given in the previous choices, lines (63), (64), and (65) in the example. Such operational situations are called *exceptions*. The meaning of line (68) is that when line (68) is executed, the system implements an error routine.

4.2. Loops

Loops are iteration statements and they are the same in Ada language as in any other programming language. A loop is a series of statements to be executed and reexecuted one or more times before control moves to the next statement. To control the number of times the computer executes the loop, a test condition is set up. Each time the loop is executed, the computer checks the condition. Control passes to the next statement when the condition is satisfied.

4.2.1. The Basic Loop

The basic loop statement in Ada is illustrated by lines (70) through (74).

```
X := 1;                            (70)
loop                               (71)
    X := X+1;                      (72)
    exit when X = 50;              (73)
end loop;                          (74)
```

The above program segment tells the computer to add 1 to *X* until the sum equals 50, then to exit the loop. Note that the condition—line (73)—is within the loop. The use of **exit** is discussed in detail in Section 4.3.1.

4.2.2. The For Loop

Lines (76) through (78) illustrate the operation of a standard **for** loop, controlled by a **for** statement.

```
TOTAL := 0;                        (75)
for I in 1 . . 25 loop             (76)
    TOTAL := TOTAL+CASH(I);        (77)
end loop;                          (78)
```

The loop sums twenty-five elements of an array called CASH; and it comprises lines (76) through (78). The program executes the loop twenty-five times; therefore, the assignment statement on line (77) executes twenty-five times. After the twenty-fifth loop, control passes to line (78) and the loop terminates. If needed for a special situation, Ada also provides the ability to increment in reverse, e.g., using the above example, from 25 down to 1.

4.2.3. The While Loop

The next program segment demonstrates a loop controlled by the **while** condition.

```
while GAS_IN_TANK+0.1 <= TANK_SIZE              (79)
   loop                                          (80)
      PUMP_GAS;   - -   This step adds 0.1 gallon. (81)
      GAS_IN_TANK := GAS_IN_TANK + 0.1;          (82)
      other statements;                          (83)
   end loop;                                      (84)
```

The **while** loop is controlled by the boolean condition stated in line (79), which is tested before each execution of the basic loop. The loop terminates when the **while** clause evaluates as false.

4.3. Control Statements

In all programming languages there are a number of statements that are generally lumped together under the control category. The most common are exit statements, labels, goto statements, call statements, return statements, pragmas, and exceptions.

4.3.1. The Exit Statement

Depending on the truth value of a condition, an **exit** statement may cause the termination of a loop. An example follows:

```
Y := 0;                                          (85)
for I in 1 . . MAX_NUM_ITEMS loop                (86)
   GET_NEW_ITEM(NEW_ITEM);                        (87)
   MERGE_ITEM(NEW_ITEM, STORAGE_FILE);           (88)
   exit when NEW_ITEM = TERMINAL_ITEM;           (89)
end loop;                                         (90)
```

When the condition stated in line (89) occurs, looping is terminated and program execution passes to line (90), which ends the
loop.

Control statements may be nested as the following example—a
for loop with a nested **while** loop—illustrates in lines (91) through
(98).

Y := 0;	(91)
for X **in** 1 . . 25 **loop**	(92)
while B(X) >= 0 **loop**	(93)
Y := 1+B(X);	(94)
exit when Y = 20;	(95)
end loop;	(96)
exit when Y = 20;	(97)
end loop;	(98)

The illustration provides exit from the inner loop when Y = 20;
it also provides exit from the outer loop when the same condition,
Y = 20, holds.

4.3.2. Labels

Labels are useful in control situations. Statements are labeled so
that they may be referenced in **goto** statements. Ada statements
may be labeled with identifiers enclosed by double brackets, for
example:

⟪COMPARE⟫	(99)

Line (99) creates a label identifyng a previously defined program
entity. Section 4.3.3 below, the **goto** statement, includes an illustration of the use of labels.

4.3.3. The goto Statement

In common with other languages, the execution of a **goto** statement
results in the transfer of control to another statement specified
by a label. For example:

if A(K) = B **then**	(100)
C := A(K);	(101)
goto COMPARE;	(102)
end if:	(103)

Sequence of statements;   (104)
COMPARE : D := F;   (105)

The **goto** statement specifying a label is line (102). The label is
COMPARE. Note that in this application the label is not enclosed
by double brackets as in line (99); double brackets are only used
when the label is created.

Good programming techniques discourage the use of **goto** statements. This is because **goto** statements are hard to debug. As a
result, they tend to introduce errors. In Ada, the **goto** is very restric-
tive. A **goto** statement cannot transfer control out of a program
module. The inverse is also true. A **goto** cannot transfer control
from outside a program module into that unit.

4.3.4. Call Statements

Though call is not a reserved word in Ada, the language provides
for the use of call statements in program modules. By definition,
a call is either a procedure call or a function call. It will be remem-
bered that there are two subprogram categories, procedures and
functions.

Procedures may or may not have parameters. If we wish to call
a parameterless procedure, the method is to enter only the procedure name followed by a semicolon. The word *call* is not required.
For example, assume we have a procedure named SORT. To perform
a procedure call, we write:

SORT;   (106)

Line (106) is a call without parameters. As an example of a call
for a procedure with parameters, we write:

UP_DATE(A,B,D);   (107)

This example calls procedure UP_DATE with parameters A, B,
and D.

The practical value of the call is illustrated by the example in
Chapter 7, which discusses tasks; in the presentation of packages
in Chapter 8; and throughout Part 2 of this book.

4.3.5. The Return Statement

The **return** statement terminates the execution of a function, procedure, or **accept** statement, and it also indicates the completion of

a subprogram call. It cannot appear within a function body or a procedure body. A **return** statement for a function must include an expression whose value is the result calculated by the function, and it must be of the type specified in the **return** clause of the function specification. Finally, a **return** statement cannot transfer control out of a program unit.

For a procedure the **return** statement is written as:

   return;   (108)

In the case of a function, the return statement is written as:

   return KEY_VALUE(LAST_INDEX);   (109)

In line (109) the identifier KEY_VALUE, is the name of the function. The practical use of the **return** statement is illustrated in Chapter 6, which introduces subprograms.

4.3.6. Pragmas and Exceptions

The special controls, pragmas and exceptions, are explained in Chapter 9.

5

Arrays

5.0. Arrays, Definition

In many instances, it is convenient to represent a list of items of the same type by a single identifier. Individual items are distinguished by an index, usually an integer. Such a data structure is called an **array.** Arrays are one-dimensional or two-dimensional. A row of numbers is an example of a one-dimensional array. A table is an example of a two-dimensional array.

5.1. Array Specification

Inasmuch as an array is a data structure, it must be typed. Array type definitions are named in type declarations as explained in Chapter 3. Line (110) illustrates:

    type WEEK_DAY **is array** (1 . . 7) **of** INTEGER;   (110)

The above defines an array seven components long of **type** IN-TEGER and named WEEK_DAY. It is similar to the composite **type** declarations in Chapter 3, Section 3.1.3. INTEGER is predefined.

An object of the array defined in line (110) is declared in this way:

    HOURS_WORKED : WEEK_DAY;   (111)

The object, HOURS_WORKED, is a variable.

5.2. Array Notation

Array notation in Ada is similar to that of other high-level languages. Each component in an array is identified by an index number called a *subscript*. In the example array, line (110), the indices are numbers 1 through 7. Inasmuch as individual items—technically, data elements—in an array are distinguished from one another by a subscript index, we may designate a particular element in this manner:

HOURS_WORKED(6);   (113)

Line (113) identifies a specific place in the array, location 6. Note that line (113) does not say what is in location 6.

The notation technique described above is applicable to two-dimensional arrays as well. A table consisting of rows and columns is an example of a two-dimensional array. We designate a particular element of a table as:

A(11,5);   (114)

Line (114) designates the element in the eleventh row of the fifth column of array A. A two-dimensional array is commonly called a *matrix*.

5.3. Array Operations

Array operations are handled in Ada in essentially the same manner as in other languages. We assign data to specific array locations using an assignment statement. For example, with the array WEEK_DAY and the object declared in line (111), assume that ten hours are worked on day 6, and further, assume that we wish to assign ten hours to location 6. The assignment statement will read:

HOURS_WORKED(6) := 10;   (115)

The following example shows how to assign data to every location in an array. We again use array WEEK_DAY specified in line (110). For the example, we assume we wish to assign the following hours to the array:

Hours worked	Day of the week
0	1
8	2
8	3
10	4
12	5
10	6
0	7

The hours are assigned in this way:

HOURS_WORKED := (0,8,8,10,12,10,0);   (116)

In line (116), the hours worked each day of the week are assigned to the variable, HOURS_WORKED. Each entry is automatically subscripted with an index number that corresponds to the appropriate day of the week.

We may wish to assign a single item in an array to a variable. To illustrate, assume that we wish to assign the hours worked on day 5 to a variable TIME; also assume that TIME is already typed. We write the assignment statement as follows:

TIME := HOURS_WORKED(5);   (117)

Line (117) assigns the hours worked on the fifth day of the week to TIME. Note that the assignment statements, line (115) and line (117), do not state how many elements are in the array; the statements designate specific elements of the array.

Any legal Ada operation—addition, subtraction, multiplication, division, and exponentiation—may be performed on the elements of an array. For example, if we have two arrays—say A and B— we could write:

C := A(3)+B(4);   (118)

The third element of A is added to the fourth element of B and the result is assigned to variable C.

As another example:

C := A(5)*2;   (119)

The fifth element of A is multiplied by 2, and the result is assigned to variable C.

5.4. Strings

In common with other languages, the string is the basic Ada program entity for handling text. By definition, a *string* is a one-dimensional array in which all components are characters.

STRING is a predefined array type in the Ada language; it comprises character components and integer indices. When declaring a string, programmers must specify the minimum length; a string may be as short as one character. The format of a string declaration is:

> **type** STRING **is array**(NATURAL **range** <>)
>
> **of** CHARACTER;   (120)

Data items declared as a string may look like this:

> PRESIDENT : STRING(1 . . 10);   (121)

This declares PRESIDENT as a variable of the predefined type STRING, which is 10 characters long.

Multiple object declarations may also be made. For example, we can say:

> FIRST_NAME,LAST_NAME : STRING(1 . . 15);   (122)

Text assigned to a string variable is enclosed in double quotation marks. In the case of the object declaration in line (121), we can write:

> PRESIDENT := "Washington";   (123)

For multiple declarations per line (122), we can write:

> FIRST_NAME,LAST_NAME := "Evelyn Kaufmann";   (124)

In the examples, lines (123) and (124), the length of the text exactly equaled the space reserved by the object declarations. This is important. If the length of text exceeded the reserved space, the compiler would have rejected the text at compilation time.

6

Subprograms

6.0. Subprograms

As pointed out in Chapter 2, the subprogram is one of the basic program units in the Ada Language System. A subprogram consists of a specification part and an action part and is invoked by a subprogram call. Subprograms are either procedures or functions. As noted in Chapter 2, procedures perform an action; a null is considered an action. Functions also perform an action, but in addition, functions return a result.

Let us first consider procedures, then functions.

6.1. Procedures

The general format for a procedure is:

procedure NAME (parameter specifications) **is**	(125)
(local declarations);	(126)
begin	(127)
(sequence of statements);	(128)
end (NAME);	(129)

Lines (125) and (126) comprise the specification section of the subprogram unit, lines (127) through (129) the body or action part.

Following is an example subprogram—a sort procedure—that implements the above format and illustrates a number of Ada programming principles. It will be noted that the procedure is indented in accordance with the practice of structured programming. This facilitates reading and checking. Similarities to PL/1 and other modern high-level languages will also be noted.

```
type INDEX is range 1 . . 500;                    (130)
type VECTOR is array (INDEX range <>)
                             of INTEGER;          (131)
     --   the symbol <> means an unspecified range.
procedure SORT (A : in out VECTOR) is             (132)
  J : INDEX;                                       (133)
  TEMP : INTEGER;                                  (134)

begin                                              (135)
  for                                              (136)
    I in A'FIRST . . A'LAST                        (137)
  loop                                             (138)
    J := I;                                        (139)
    while                                          (140)
      J < A'LAST                                   (141)
    loop                                           (142)
      J := J+1;                                    (143)
      if                                           (144)
        A(I) > A(J);                               (145)
      then                                         (146)
        TEMP := A(I);                              (147)
        A(I) := A(J);                              (148)
        A(J) := TEMP;                              (149)
    end loop;                                      (150)
  end loop;                                        (151)
end SORT;                                          (152)
```

In this example, the specification part includes lines (132) through (134), the action part, lines (135) through (152). Note that the type declarations—lines (130) and (131)—are stated outside of the actual procedure.

The procedure module has one formal parameter, array A, declared in line (132) as an object having the attributes of the array named VECTOR and defined in the type statement on line (131). In other words, the definition of VECTOR on line (131) describes the attributes of A.

The reserved words, **in out** appearing in line (132) refer to input to and output from the procedures of array A. The words are predefined in the INPUT-OUTPUT package. Chapter 10 covers the meaning in detail.

Local variables are declared on lines (133) and (134). TEMP is a variable declared to have the attributes of the predefined variable INTEGER. It is used as temporary storage for any component of the array. The variable J, declared to be of the predefined INDEX type, is used as a counter for subscripting the components of array A.

The action part of the example, the body of the subprogram, includes three nested structures that control the order of execution. There are two loop statements controlling the repetition of the action and an **if** control structure selecting among alternative actions. The outer loop structure is a **for** loop specifying and implicitly declaring a control variable I, which varies sequentially from the first, or lowest (A'FIRST), to the last, or highest (A'LAST), component in the array. In the final pass, the smallest number in the array will be first, the largest last.

6.2. Functions

By definition, a **function** is a subprogram that returns a value or result. Like other Ada program entities, the function consists of two parts, a specification part and a body. The function specification is similar to that of a procedure; only the first line is different. The format of the first line is:

function IDENTIFIER(PARAMETER_LIST) **return**
TYPE_OF_RESULT;   (153)

Inasmuch as functions return a value, the specification must include the reserved word **return**. The **return** is followed by an expression that gives the value to be returned.

Following is an example function that sequentially adds the numbers that comprise each component of an array and then assigns the total to the variable SUM.

```
type VECTOR is array(INTEGER range <>) of REAL; (154)
function SUMMATION(X : VECTOR) return REAL is  (155)
                          SUM : REAL := 0;   (156)
begin                                         (157)
   for I in X' range loop                     (158)
```

SUM := SUM + X(I);	(159)
end loop;	(160)
return SUM;	(161)
end SUMMATION;	(162)

Line (154) types the identifier VECTOR as an array comprised of real integer numbers.

Lines (155) and (156) are the function specification. In line (155), the components of the array VECTOR are declared; line (156) declares the variable SUM, types it as a real number, and initially assigns it a value of zero.

Lines (157) through (162) comprise the body of the function. Line (158) sets up a loop that will run through all components of the array. In line (159), the values of X are added to the previous value of SUM, then SUM is assigned a new value. Line (160) terminates the loop when the last component of X is added.

6.3. Overloading

From time to time, situations may arise in which the same identifier is used in several different specifications within the same subprogram module. For example, we may have two subprograms that look like this:

procedure PUT(X : INTEGER);	(163)
procedure PUT(X : STRING);	(164)

If the procedures given on lines (163) and (164) are used in the same program module, an ambiguous situation is created. The same identifier, X, is used for both integer numbers and text material. In such a situation, the compiler would not know how to handle the identifiers. This phenomenon is called *overloading*.

Other overload situations may not always be as obvious as this instance. For example:

type NEWSPAPER **is** (SUN, TIMES, TRIBUNE, PRESS,	
DISPATCH);	(165)
type SOLAR_SYSTEM **is** (SUN, MOON, VENUS, MARS,	
NEPTUNE, MERCURY, SATURN, PLUTO, URANUS);	(166)

Based on line (165) we can write the declaration:

JOURNAL : NEWSPAPER;	(167)

Line (167) declares JOURNAL to be an object having the attributes of NEWSPAPER. At a later point we may write the assignment statement:

JOURNAL := SUN; (168)

In line (168), the identifier, SUN, obviously refers to a newspaper. We typed it in line (165). But in line (166), we typed SUN as a component of the SOLAR SYSTEM. Thus an ambiguity is created, and the program entity is said to be overloaded.

There are a number of ways to handle overloading. As an example, in the case of the overloading shown in line (168) and caused by lines (165) and (166), we can be more explicit in the name of the newspaper. If SUN refers to say the *Clay County Sun,* we could rewrite line (163) as:

type NEWSPAPER **is** (CC_SUN, TIMES, TRIBUNE,
                         PRESS, DISPATCH); (169)

What we have done is tie the name SUN to a specific newspaper. In summary, overloading can and does occur from time to time. It is programmer controlled.

Chapter

7

Tasks

7.0. Tasks

As stated in Chapter 2, tasks are program entities that may execute
in parallel. Stated another way, tasks provide facilities for the parallel execution of subprocesses of a main program module. Tasks may
execute on multicomputer configurations, or they may interleave
on a single computer. They are not independent program units,
but are nested entities and operate within Ada program modules,
i.e., procedures and or packages. Figure 7.1 illustrates this principle.

This figure shows the relationship between four tasks—BETA,
GAMMA, EPSILON, and OMEGA— all nested within procedure
ALPHA. Procedure ALPHA is called the *parent;* the four tasks
are known as *siblings.* Some writers would refer to the four tasks
as *threads.* In general, whenever the parent is executed, all siblings
are executed. Thus in Figure 7.1, the four sibling tasks execute

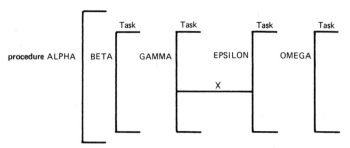

Figure 7.1 Tasks nested within the procedure ALPHA.

parallel with one another, or concurrently, when the procedure ALPHA executes. However, the four tasks—threads if you wish— are almost never the same length. Therefore, some tasks may finish before others. In this event, the task that finishes first will wait for all other tasks to finish; then the procedure will continue.

From time to time tasks may wish to communicate with one another and exchange data. As figure 7.1 illustrates, tasks GAMMA and EPSILON synchronize executions, communicate, and meet at point X. This meeting of the two tasks is referred to as a *rendezvous*. The manner in which tasks meet and communicate is discussed in Section 7.1.3 of this chapter.

The operational concept of the task is important from a hardware standpoint. Figure 7.2 illustrates. Here, we implement the four tasks in separate microprocessors. The separate microprocessors may be immediately adjacent, or they may be far apart. Nevertheless, they are still under the control of **procedure** ALPHA and may communicate with one another as required. As this discussion suggests, tasks are well suited to distributed processing.

7.1. Task Structure

Tasks, like other program units, are divided into a specification part that specifies the resources and a body that defines the implementation. The task specification is visible to other program units; the body is not. Statements already discussed in this book, supplemented by real-time synchronization commands, are used to construct tasks. Additional task control statements that implement

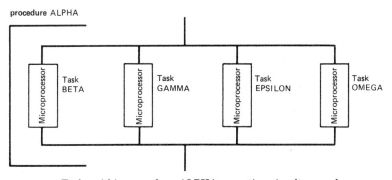

Figure 7.2 Tasks within procedure ALPHA executing simultaneously.

real-time task operations but not yet discussed in this text are the entry, the accept, the select, and the delay statements.

7.1.1. The Entry

The entry statement and a companion accept command are the primary means of communication and synchronization between tasks that operate concurrently. In Figure 7.1, the entry and accept commands implement the rendezvous and permit data to be exchanged between the two tasks. This section deals with the entry; Section 7.1.2 covers the accept.

An entry statement calls for a service. The entry is written in the specification portion of the called task. In format, it is similar to a procedure call, but operationally there is an important difference: Procedure calls immediately invoke the called procedure; entry calls cannot execute until there is synchronization with an accept statement in the called task. The format of an entry statement is:

> **entry** identifier [(discrete_range)][formal_part];   (170)

Each entry must operate with a companion accept command.

7.1.2. The Accept

The accept command provides the service called for by the entry. As previously stated, the entry is in the specification portion of the called task; the accept is in the body of that task. The format of the accept is:

> **accept** entry_name[formal_part][do   (171)
>   sequence_of_statements;   (172)
>   **end** [identifier]];   (173)

At this point, further discussion of the mechanism of task communication will be helpful.

7.1.3. The Rendezvous

For two tasks to rendezvous and exchange data, the following events must occur:

1. The task that wants to communicate—pass data to a second task—must call the second task by calling an entry in the specifi-

cation of the second task. The first task is known as the *calling task*.

2. The second task—the *called task*—accepts the call with an accept in the task body. The rendezvous does not take place until execution of the second task reaches the accept. At this point the rendezvous takes place and data is exchanged.

Figure 7.3 illustrates the operation just described.

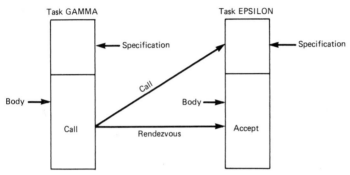

Figure 7.3   Mechanism of task communication. (1) Task GAMMA passes data to task EPSILON, (2) task GAMMA calls task EPSILON, and (3) data are passed when EPSILON reaches an **accept** command in the task body. This is the point of rendezvous.

Note the following points:

- When the first task executes the call statement, it goes into a wait state pending the rendezvous.
- The second task will not execute the accept and thus set up the rendezvous until it executes all preceding statements in the task body.

7.1.4. Example Task Implementation

The following example implements **procedure** ALPHA illustrated by Figure 7.1. It shows how tasks are implemented, how they interoperate, and how they rendezvous.

```
    procedure ALPHA is                                    (174)
        task BETA;  -- specification                      (175)
        task GAMMA;  -- specification                     (176)
        task EPSILON is                                   (177)
            entry (name of entry);  -- called by calling task   (178)
```

```
    end EPSILON;                                        (179)
    task OMEGA;  -- specification                       (180)
    task body BETA is                                   (181)
      local declarations;                               (182)
    begin                                               (183)
      series of statements;                             (184)
    end BETA;                                           (185)
    task body GAMMA is                                  (186)
      local declarations;                               (187)
    begin                                               (188)
      series of statements;                             (189)
      EPSILON (name of entry);                          (190)
      series of statements;                             (191)
    end GAMMA;                                          (192)
    task body EPSILON is                                (193)
      local declarations;                               (194)
    begin                                               (195)
      series of statements;                             (196)
      accept (name of entry);  --  accepts entry call   (197)
      series of statements;                             (198)
    end EPSILON;                                        (199)
    task body OMEGA is                                  (200)
      local declarations;                               (201)
    begin                                               (202)
      series of statements;                             (203)
    end OMEGA;                                          (204)
  begin                                                 (205)
    series of statements;                               (206)
  end procedure;                                        (207)
```

Lines (174) through (192) represent the specification portion of the procedure. The body falls between lines (193) and (207). An entry statement is declared on line (178) as part of the specification of task EPSILON.

On line (197) the **accept** in the body of task EPSILON accepts the **entry** in the EPSILON specification. EPSILON is the identifier of the task with which GAMMA wishes to communicate. Note that the call from GAMMA consists of stating the identifier name and the entry name. When GAMMA makes the call to EPSILON, line (190), GAMMA suspends execution pending action by EPSILON.

The **accept** statement on line (197) in the body of EPSILON does not accept the **entry** and execute until all preceding statements in the task body are executed. When the **accept** statement accepts the **entry**, GAMMA and EPSILON synchronize. The series of statements under the **accept**, line (198) in the example, execute and data is exchanged. This process is known as the rendezvous. When the statements under the **accept** are executed and data is exchanged, the rendezvous is terminated. The two tasks then separate and proceed with their independent and parallel executions.

7.2. Select Statements

To this point we have discussed only deterministic operations, in which each action is determined by a specific previous action. In many situations computer programs operate in a nondeterministic manner. We cannot predict at what point in time specific actions that determine the sequence of operations will take place. In other words, events that trigger actions occur on a random basis. If uncontrolled, this leads to erroneous operations. Ada copes with the problem by implementing a family of commands called *select statements*. Three selects are discussed here.

7.2.1. Select Wait

The **select** wait allows a combination of waiting for and selection of one or more alternatives. The statement looks like this:

select	(208)
[**when** condition =>]	(209)
select_alternative;	(210)
or	(211)
[**when** condition =>]	(212)
select_alternative;	(213)
end select;	(214)

The program segment may contain any number of **or** alternatives. Under the reserved word **select**, line (208), or alternatively under the reserved word **or**, line (211), action must take place. If the program is not ready for action under the **when** conditions imposed on either line (209) or (212), program execution will stop and an indefinite wait will occur.

The indefinite wait problem is solved by using the reserved word
else, as shown by the following segment.

select	(215)
[**when** condition =>]	(216)
select_alternative;	(217)
or	(218)
[**when** condition =>]	(219)
select_alternative;	(220)
else	(221)
sequence of statements;	(222)
end select;	(223)

If none of the **when** conditions are satisfied, lines (216) and (217),
the reserved word **else**, on line (221) provides access to a sequence
of statements which permit the program to proceed without delay.
As we have previously stated, there may be any number of **or** alternatives; however, only one **else** selection is permitted.

7.2.2. Conditional Select

From time to time random events may cause a number of tasks
to call the same **entry**, and the task called at the **entry** may not
be ready to rendezvous. The result is that calling tasks stop execution and queue. This situation is handled by the conditional select
command.

select	(224)
accept (NAME) do	(225)
sequence of statements;	(226)
end;	(227)
else	(228)
alternative actions;	(229)
end select;	(230)

In the above example, the **entry** will be accepted at line (225)
if the task is ready to rendezvous; if not ready, the alternative
actions provided under the reserved word **else** on line (228) will
be executed.

The programmer may wish to delay action if the **accept** on line
(225) is not ready for the **entry**. He may wish to delay for an arbi-
trary length of time, then take alternative action if the **accept** is
still not ready. The delay command permits this.

7.2.3. Select Delay

The delay command is used with the select statement. It permits programmers to artificially control the sequence of program execution by timed delays. In practice, the delay is a technique for achieving timed control of a program. Delays are expressed in seconds. Delay commands are written in this manner:

delay 4.0;   (231)

The above says: Delay program execution by four seconds.

Here's how we might wish to implement the delay in the example shown under the conditional select, lines (224) through (230).

```
select                                          (232)
    accept (NAME) do                            (233)
        sequence of statements;                 (234)
    end;                                        (235)
or                                              (236)
    delay 2.0;                                  (237)
        sequence of statements;                 (238)
end select;                                      (239)
```

The example shown in lines (232) through (239) says that if the task containing the entry NAME is ready for action and no entry call is received, the program segment waits two seconds for a call, then continues with the sequence of statements reepresented by line (238).

Chapter

8

Packages

8.0. The Package

The package is one of the program units or modules from which overall programs are constructed. The other units are subprograms and tasks, both of which have already been discussed.

Packages are a collection of logically related program entities grouped or "packaged" together. Fundamentally, packages represent pools of common data, related programs, and type declarations. Stated another way, packages bundle groups of related software entities, such as types, objects, subprograms, procedures, and tasks. From an operational standpoint, packages provide the means for treating a collection of program entities as a single unit.

Like other program entities, packages generally consist of two separate parts, the specification part and the body, or action part. The specification and the body may reside in separate library files; they may be compiled separately and at different times.

The package body is not visible to users; only the specification is visible. The black box approach is a convenient way to look at the package. In this concept, resources are packaged in a black box, and components are made available to users. When the user calls a package out of an existing library file, that person sees only the specification, i.e., the interface with the outside world. The interior of the black box—the package body—is not visible.

Though we have just made the point that packages generally consist of a specification part and a body part, this need not always be the case. In its simplest form, that representing a pool of data and types, a package body is not required.

8.1. The Package Specification

The specification is the declarative or visible part of the package. In essence, the specification is a tabulation of declarations. It lists resources available to a user. The specification contains all the information that a user needs to know or is permitted to know about the package. In its simplest form, the format of a package specification is:

package identifier **is**	(241)
declarative items;	(242)
end identifier;	(243)

It should be noted that the above format is similar to that of subprograms.

8.1.1. Example Package Specification

In Section 8.0 it was noted that if a package represents only a pool of data and types, a body is not required. Here is an example of such a package specification.

package WORK_DATA **is**	(244)
type DAY **is** (MON, TUE, WED, THU, FRI,	
SAT, SUN);	(245)
type HOURS_SPENT **is delta** 0.01 **range** 0.0 . . 24.0;	(246)
type TABLE **is array** (DAY) **of** HOURS_SPENT;	(247)
WORK_HOURS : TABLE;	(248)
NORMAL_HOURS : **constant** TABLE := (MON . . FRI =>	
8.0,SAT SUN => 0.0);	(249)
end WORK_DATA;	(250)

In this example, the specification comprises a series of type statements and object declarations. The value of the example package specification is that it provides access to information.

8.2. The Package Body

The package body is the active part of the package program unit; it implements the specification. The format is:

```
package body identifier is                          (251)
    declarations;                                   (252)
begin                                               (253)
    sequence of statements;                         (254)
end identifier;                                     (255)
```

The above format is similar to that of other Ada program entities. The package body, like the specification, is stored in library files. Unlike the specification, the body cannot be accessed by users; its only interface with users is via the specification.

8.3. Example Package

Following is an example package specification, the purpose of which is to manage inventory records. The package specification comprises lines (256) through (268).

```
package INVENTORY is                                (256)
   type ITEM is                                     (257)
      record                                        (258)
         INV_NUMBER : INTEGER range 0 . . 9;        (259)
         ITEM_CODE : INTEGER range 0 . . 7;         (260)
         QUANTITY : INTEGER range
                        0 . . INTEGER'LAST;         (261)
         ITEM_TYPE : CHARACTER;                     (262)
      end record;                                   (263)
   NULL_ITEM : constant ITEM := (INV_NUMBER|
ITEM_CODE|QUANTITY => 0, ITEM_TYPE => ' ');         (264)
   procedure INSERT (NEW_ITEM : in ITEM);           (265)
   procedure RETRIEVE (FIRST_ITEM : out ITEM);      (266)
   FILE_FULL exception;  --   may be raised by insert
                                    procedure       (267)
end INVENTORY;                                      (268)
```

The above specification contains both type specifications and object declarations. INTEGER and CHARACTER are predefined. The **procedure** INSERT provides a way to insert new inventory items into the file. The **procedure** RETRIEVE provides a technique for removing items from inventory. The reserved words **in** and **out** in lines (265) and (266) provide the means for inserting new items in the inventory file or for removing old items. The methodology will be more fully explained in Chapter 10, "Input-Output." The use of the reserved word **exception**, line (267), is explained in Chapter 9.

The body of the INVENTORY package looks like this:

```
package body INVENTORY is                               (269)
   SIZE : constant INTEGER := 10000;                    (270)
   subtype INDEX is INTEGER range 0 . . SIZE;           (271)
   type INTERNAL_ITEM is                                (272)
   record                                               (273)
      CONTENT : ITEM;                                   (274)
      NEXT_ITEM : INDEX;                                (275)
      PREV_ITEM : INDEX;                                (276)
   end record;                                          (277)
   TABLE: array (INDEX) of INTERNAL_ITEM;               (278)
   FIRST_FREE_ITEM : INDEX := 1;                        (279)
   FIRST_BUSY_ITEM : INDEX := 0;                        (280)
   function FREELIST_EMPTY return BOOLEAN
                                     is . . end;        (281)
   function BUSYLIST_EMPTY return BOOLEAN
                                     is . . end;        (282)
   procedure EXCHANGE (FROM,TO : in INDEX)
                                     is . . end;        (283)
   procedure INSERT(NEW_ITEM: in ITEM) is . . end;      (284)
   begin                                                (285)
   if                                                   (286)
      FREELIST_EMPTY;                                   (287)
   then                                                 (288)
      raise NO_MORE_ROOM;                               (289)
   end if;                                              (290)
   --   remaining code for INSERT                       (291)
end INSERT;                                             (292)
   procedure RETRIEVE (FIRST_ITEM : out ITEM)
                                     is . . end;        (293)
   begin                                                (294)
   --   code for initialization of table of linkages    (295)
```

```
      --   for both the free list and the busy list        (296)
    end INVENTORY;                                          (297)
```

8.4. The Reserved Word Private

In the example package specification shown in lines (256) through (268) and more fundamentally, as defined by the specification format in lines (241) through (243), users may access the components of the specification and change them. If the specification is a standard library package, we want to prevent changes. The reserved word **private** in the specification provides the mechanism. The following specification format illustrates.

```
    package identifier is                                  (298)
      declarative items;                                   (299)
    private                                                (300)
      declarative items;                                   (301)
    end identifier;                                        (302)
```

Lines (298) through (302) are identical to the format shown in lines (241) through (243) except for the addition of the reserved word **private**, and the declarative items listed under it.

The reserved word **private** implements a technique to hide from users the details of the program segment that is declared under it, line (301) in the example. Like other type declarations, private types define a set of values and a collection of applicable operations. However, unlike other types, the structural details of private types are not visible or available to users. The practical effect is to protect the operational details of that segment from outside interference. In other words, users cannot change the code. Use of the **private** type specification is not required; it is optional.

8.4.1. Example Package Specification Using the Private Type

The following Ada package specification illustrates how a group of file handling subprograms is packaged using the **private** type.

```
    package I_O_PACKAGE is                                 (303)
      type FILE_NAME is private;                           (304)
      procedure OPEN(F : in out FILE_NAME);                (305)
      procedure CLOSE(F : in out FILE_NAME);               (306)
```

```
procedure READ(F : in FILE_NAME; ITEM :
                   out INTEGER);        (307)
procedure WRITE(F : in FILE_NAME; ITEM :
                   in INTEGER);         (308)
   private                              (309)
      type FILE_NAME is                 (310)
         record                         (311)
            INTERNAL_NAME : INTEGER := 0;   (312)
         end record;                    (313)
end I_O_PACKAGE;                        (314)
```

In line (304) we first declare the identifier FILE_NAME and note that it is private. We use the reserved word in line (309), and then in subsequent lines we further define the identifier. This information on an identifier is not visible to a user. Use of the reserved word **private** has no impact on the body of the package.

8.5. Package Access

We have already noted that packages are collections of logically related entities. We have also noted that the body of a package is not visible to other program units. The specification provides the interface to the outside world; the specification is visible to other program entities.

Access to library packages is via the specification. In the process of program compilation, existing packages filed in program libraries may be accessed through the specification of other compilation units by implementing the **with** and **use** clauses.

8.5.1. The With and the Use Clauses

The **with** clause is used to specify the library packages to be made visible within another compilation unit. The effect of the clause is to permit the library packages to be used as additional program entities in the new unit. Within the new compilation unit, the **use** clause gives the name of the library package. The following example, which shows how to implement the **with** and **use** clauses, will clarify.

```
with INVENTORY;  -- library unit     (315)
procedure RECORD_UPDATE is           (316)
```

use INVENTORY;	(317)
declarative items;	(318)
begin	(319)
sequence of statements;	(320)
end;	(321)

In the above example, lines (315) through (321), the name of the new program compilation unit is RECORD_UPDATE; it is written as a procedure. INVENTORY is the name of the library package. RECORD_UPDATE uses the procedure INVENTORY. Note that the **with** INVENTORY statement is placed outside of the procedure; the **use** INVENTORY statement is placed at the beginning of the declarative section of the procedure RECORD_UPDATE. Its function is to permit the INVENTORY library entity to be used in the RECORD_UPDATE program.

9

Pragmas and Exceptions

9.0. Pragmas

By definition, a **pragma** is an instruction to the compiler. It is also a vehicle that conveys information to the compiler. In a sense, the pragma permits the programmer to talk to the compiler and, in so doing, to cause the compiler to perform certain operations requested by the programmer.

Pragmas are written into Ada program units. The location of the pragma within the program unit depends on the pragma. In some cases the pragma must appear at the beginning of the actual program unit, in other cases, wherever a declaration or a statement is permitted.

In a program unit, the pragma is introduced by the reserved word **pragma**, which is then followed by the identifier and pertinent arguments. The format of the pragma is:

pragma ::= **pragma** [(argument [,argument])];   (322)

Pragmas are either predefined in the Ada language or implementation defined.

9.1. What a Pragma does

What a pragma does is best explained by means of examples. Following are two examples of the use of predefined pragmas.

9.1.1. Examples of Predefined Pragmas

One of the predefined Ada pragmas establishes random access memory (RAM) size. The pragma looks like this:

    pragma MEMORY_SIZE (64000);   (323)

Line (323) establishes the required memory size as 64,000 units. In other words, 64,000 bytes of RAM must be reserved for this program. This pragma can appear only at the beginning of a program module.

Another example of a predefined pragma is the following:

    pragma LIST(OFF);   (324)

Line (324) suspends listing of a program entity.

9.2. Predefined Pragmas

There are thirteen predefined pragmas in the Ada language:

Pragma	*Definition*
CONTROLLED	Specifies that automatic storage reclamation should not be performed for objects of the access type except upon leaving the scope of the access type definition.
ELABORATE	Takes the simple name of a secondary unit as the single argument. Allowed immediately after the context clause of a compilation unit; the argument must denote a secondary unit that is the body of a library unit mentioned in the context clause.
INLINE	Takes a list of subprogram names as arguments. It appears in the same declarative part as the named subprograms. Provides that the named subprogram bodies should be expanded inline at each call.
LIST	Takes ON or OFF as argument. It can appear any where. It provides that listing of the program unit is to be continued or suspended until a LIST pragma with the opposite argument is given.
MEMORY_SIZE	Takes an integer number as argument. It can appear only before a library unit. It establishes the available number of storage units in memory.

OPTIMIZE	Uses as arguments, TIME or SPACE. Specifies whether time or space is the primary optimization criterion.
PACK	Takes a record or type name as argument. It specifies that storage minimization should be the main criterion when selecting the representation of a given type.
PAGE	Specifies that the program text which follows should start on a new page if the compiler is producing a listing.
PRIORITY	Specifies the priority of a task. It must appear in a task specification or the outer-declarative part of the main program.
SHARED	Takes the simple name of a variable as the single argument. It is allowed for a variable declared by object declaration whose type is scalar or access. Specifies that every read or update for the variable is a synchronization point.
STORAGE_UNIT	Takes an integer as an argument; it appears only before a library unit. It establishes the number of bits per storage unit.
SUPPRESS	This pragma takes a check name; it appears in the declarative part of a program unit. The pragma specifies that the designated check is suppressed in that unit.
SYSTEM_NAME	Takes a name as an argument; it appears only before a library unit. The pragma establishes the name of the object machine.

9.3. Implementation Defined Pragmas

Implementation-defined pragmas are those pragmas that are unique to each individual implementation of Ada, i.e., to each compiler. This is a list of unique pragmas that must be provided with each Ada implementation. Implementation pragmas are compiler dependent. Therefore no single list of such pragmas exists.

9.3.1. Special Pragmas

Some specialized pragmas are not in the predefined list but are often available from vendors. A particularly interesting example is a pragma that provides an operational interface to subprograms written in other languages. This means that an Ada program segment can call a subprogram written in another language. The format of this pragma is:

pragma INTERFACE (language_name, subprogram_name);

(325)

As an example of how this pragma operates, assume we wish to call a Fortran subprogram for calculating square roots. We will also assume the name of the subprogram is SQRT. The pragma for calling the Fortran subprogram, SQRT, looks like this:

pragma INTERFACE (FORTRAN,SQRT);   (326)

In actual usage, this interface pragma must appear after the program or package specification.

9.4. Exceptions

In every computer application, operational problems—errors—may arise and in all probability, will arise. Errors are the result of unexpected events. Typical examples include an unknown program glitch, erroneous input data, hardware breakdown, damage to a sector of a disk, etc.

In some computers, program execution shuts down when an operational error occurs, because the computer has no way to handle the problem. From a practical standpoint, most users do not want to shut down when the unexpected happens. This is especially true with military computers or any computer performing control operations. The user's problem therefore is how to program the computer to handle the incident and avoid shutdown.

Ada provides a technique to handle unforeseen events. The methodology is built around a concept called handling exceptions. By definition, an *exception* is an operational event that causes suspension of normal program execution. Drawing attention to the event is called *raising* the exception. Executing some action in response to the event is known as *handling* the exception. The program segment that performs this function is called the exception *handler*. A number of exceptions are predefined by the Ada language system. Additional exceptions are programmer defined.

9.4.1. Predefined Exceptions

Predefined exceptions are:

CONSTRAINT ERROR	Occurs when a range or index constraint is violated.
NUMERIC ERROR	When the result of a predefined numeric operation does not lie within the implemented range of the numeric type; division by zero is an example.
PROGRAM ERROR	Raised when all alternatives of a select statement having no **else** part are closed. Also raised if an attempt is made to access a subprogram, package, or task prematurely.
SELECT ERROR	Happens when all alternatives of a select statement that has no else part are closed.
STORAGE ERROR	The dynamic storage assigned to a task is exceeded; or if, during execution, the available space for the collection of allocated objects is exhausted.
TASKING ERROR	Exceptions arising during intertask communication.

9.4.2. User-Defined Exception

As noted above, programmers may define exceptions. Two examples follow:

OVERFLOW : **exception**;	(327)
NO_VOLTAGE : **exception**;	(328)

The format is an identifier followed by the reserve word **exception**. Lines (327) and (328) say that if an overflow situation occurs or if a no voltage condition happens, this is an exception.

9.4.3. Exception Handlers

When an operational event defined as an exception occurs, the exception raises the handler which then responds. The handler is a program segment placed in the body of the package, subprogram, or task by the programmer. The exception handler processes exceptions as they are raised within the program module.

9.4.4. Raise Statements

As previously noted, drawing attention to the exceptional event is called raising the exception. This action automatically causes program execution to shift to the handler. In other words, when an exception is raised, normal program execution is suspended and control is transferred to the exception handler. The exception handler is called into action by the reserved word **raise**.

9.4.5. Examples of How to Implement Exceptions

Following are two examples of how to implement exceptions. The first covers the NO_VOLTAGE exception shown in line (328).

exception	(329)
when NO_VOLTAGE =>	(330)
series of statements that process a no voltage situation;	
	(331)
end;	(332)

The actions performed by lines (329) through (332) are self-evident. However, note that in line (331), a series of statements, a program segment was introduced to handle the no voltage problem. The series of statements included in the program segment introduced by line (331) is the exception handler.

The second example is built around a repeat of lines (61) through (68). Note the manner in which the exception raises an error routine.

case BIN_NUMBER(COUNT) **is**	(333)
when 1 => UPDATE_BIN(1);	(334)
when 2 => UPDATE_BIN(2);	(335)
when 3|4 =>	(336)
EMPTY_BIN(1);	(337)
EMPTY_BIN(2);	(338)
when others => **raise** ERROR;	(339)
end case;	(340)

Line (339) raises an error routine when none of conditions 1, 2, 3, and 4 occurs. ERROR is the name of the program segment.

Chapter

10

Input-Output

10.0. Introduction to Input-Output

In the Ada programming language the term *input-output* refers to the transfer of sequences of data—called files—between the computer and various external sources or destinations, i.e., peripheral devices, such as disks, printers, terminals, sensors, and communication links. In format, files resemble arrays.

Input-output operations are handled by the predefined packages listed below:

SEQUENTIAL_IO and DIRECT_IO—For input-output operations applicable to files containing elements of a single type

TEXT_IO—Applicable to text input-output readable by humans

IO_EXCEPTIONS—Defines exceptions needed by the above three packages

LOW_LEVEL_IO—Provides for direct control of peripheral devices

Before proceeding with a discussion of the above-listed predefined input-output packages, let us clarify the terminology relating to input-output operations.

10.1. Input-Output Terminology

Two kinds of access to external files are defined, sequential access and direct access. The corresponding file types and the associated operations are provided by the predefined packages, SEQUEN-TIAL_IO and DIRECT_IO. A file object to be used for sequential access is called a *sequential* file; one to be used for direct access is called a *direct* file.

For sequential access, the file is viewed as a sequence of values that are transferred in the order of their appearance as produced by the program or by the environment. When the file is opened, transfer of data starts from the beginning. An example of a sequential file is data transferred to and from a tape drive.

For direct access, the file is viewed as a set of elements occupying consecutive positions in linear order. A value can be transferred to or from an element of the file at any selected position. The position of an element is specified by its index, which is a number greater than zero. The first element, if any, has index number one; the index of the last element is called the *current size*. The current size is zero if there are no elements.

An open direct file has a current index which is the index that will be used by the next read or write operation. When a direct file is opened, the current index is set to one. The current index of a direct file is a property of the file object, not the external file. Data written to and read from a disk drive is an example application for DIRECT_IO.

Input and output processes are expressed as operations on objects of some file type. As used in this chapter, the term *file* refers to a declared object of file type. Programmers declare files and subsequently associate them with appropriate sources and destinations. The following definitions relating to declared files are used in input-output operations.

External File—Values input to the program from an environment external to the program or output to the external environment

Internal File—Object within a program that may be associated with an external file

File—Refers to the internal file

Open File—Internal file associated with an external file

Closed File—Internal file not associated with an external file

Relative to input-output, the term *file mode* or simply *mode* is frequently used. The term refers to the direction of data flow relative to the user. There are three file modes, one of which is associated with every file; the three modes are:

IN_FILE—Read only; the computer transfers data from an external file; the direction is from the external source to the computer.

OUT_FILE—Write only; data transferred from the computer to an external device; the direction is from the computer out.

INOUT_FILE—Read or write; the computer either transfers data from an external source or transfers data to an external device; the direction is either in or out.

All three of the above listed modes are allowed for direct files. The only allowable modes for sequential files are IN_FILE and OUT_FILE.

10.2. File Management

The procedures and functions described in this section provide for the control of external files. The facilities are available in the predefined packages, SEQUENTIAL_IO, DIRECT_IO, and TEXT_IO. The following procedure shows how to create an external file:

```
procedure CREATE(FILE : in out FILE_TYPE ;          (341)
    MODE : in FILE_MODE := default_mode;
    NAME : in STRING := " ";
    FORM : in STRING := " ");
```

The above procedure establishes a new external file with a specific name and form; it associates this file with a given file—a declared object of file type.

The procedure in line (342) provides for opening files.

```
procedure OPEN (FILE : in out FILE_TYPE ;           (342)
    MODE : in FILE_MODE := default_mode;
    NAME : in STRING := " ";
    FORM : in STRING := " ");
```

The above example associates a given internal file with an existing external file having the same name.

When a file has completed processing, the association of the internal file object and the external file may be severed by the CLOSE procedure.

procedure CLOSE (FILE : **in out** FILE_TYPE) ;   (343)

The effect of line (343) is to sever the association between the internal file and its associated external file.

If an external file is no longer required, it may be deleted by the procedure.

procedure DELETE(FILE : **in out** FILE_TYPE) ;   (344)

The above deletes the external file associated with a given internal file. The given file is closed.

procedure RESET(FILE : **in out** FILE_TYPE; MODE :
                         in FILE_MODE);   (345)
procedure RESET(FILE : **in out** FILE_TYPE) ;   (346)

The above procedures, lines (345) and (346) reset the given file so that reading from or writing to its elements can be restarted from the beginning of the file. For direct access, the current index is set to one. If a MODE parameter is supplied, the current mode of the given file is set to the given mode.

function MODE(FILE : **in** FILE_TYPE)
                         return FILE_MODE;   (347)

The function on line (347) returns the current mode of the given file.

function NAME(FILE : **in** FILE_TYPE)
                         return STRING;   (348)

Line (348) returns a string which identifies the external file currently associated with the given file.

function FORM(FILE : **in** FILE_TYPE)
                         return STRING;   (349)

The above function returns the form string for the external file currently associated with the given file. The returned string will correspond to a full specification.

function IS_OPEN(FILE : **in** FILE_TYPE)
                         return BOOLEAN;   (350)

The function on line (350) returns TRUE if the file is open, i.e., associated with an external file.

These procedures and functions—lines (341) through (350)—will raise the exception, STATUS_ERROR, if the file is already open. They are provided in the three predefined packages, SEQUEN-TIAL_IO, DIRECT_IO, and TEXT_IO.

10.2.1. Sequential Input-Output

The operations available for sequential input and output are described in this section. The STATUS_ERROR exception is raised if any of the following operations is attempted for a file that is not open.

procedure READ(FILE : **in** IN_FILE_TYPE; ITEM :
out ELEMENT_TYPE);   (351)

Line (351) operates on a file of mode IN_FILE; it reads an element from the given file and returns the value of this element to the ITEM parameter.

procedure WRITE(FILE : **in** FILE_TYPE; ITEM : **in**
ELEMENT_TYPE);   (352)

This procedure writes the value of ITEM to the given file. In other words data are transferred from the external file to the internal file.

function END_OF_FILE(FILE : **in** FILE_TYPE) **return**
BOOLEAN;   (353)

The END_OF_FILE function operates on a file of mode IN_FILE. It returns TRUE if no more elements can be read from the given file; otherwise it returns FALSE.

10.2.2. Direct Input-Output

The operations for direct input-output are described below. The exception, STATUS_ERROR, is raised if any operations are attempted for a file that is not open.

The predefined procedures for reading files are:

procedure READ(FILE : **in** FILE_TYPE;
ITEM : **out** ELEMENT_TYPE;
FROM : **in** POSITIVE_COUNT);   (354)

procedure READ(FILE : **in** FILE_TYPE;   ITEM :
out ELEMENT_TYPE);   (355)

Lines (354) and (355) operate on a file mode, IN_FILE or INOUT _FILE. Line (354) sets the current index of the given file to the index given by the parameter FROM. For both lines (354) and (355) the procedures return in the parameter ITEM the value of the element whose position in the given file is specified by the current index. In addition the procedures increment the current index by one.

The predefined procedures for writing to files are:

procedure WRITE(FILE : **in** FILE_TYPE;
ITEM : **in** ELEMENT_TYPE;
TO : **in** POSITIVE_COUNT);   (356)
procedure WRITE(FILE : **in** FILE_TYPE;
ITEM : **in** ELEMENT_TYPE);   (357)

The WRITE procedures shown in lines (356) and (357) operate on a file mode INOUT_FILE or OUT_FILE. Line (356) sets the index of the given file to the index value given by the parameter TO. Both lines (356) and (357) give the value of the parameter ITEM to the element whose position in the given file is specified by the current index of the file. In addition the procedures increment the current index by one.

This next procedure operates on a file of any mode. It sets the current index of the given file to the given index value.

procedure SET_INDEX(FILE : **in** FILE_TYPE;
TO : **in** POSITIVE_COUNT);   (358)

Line (359), below, returns the current index of the given file; it operates on a file of any mode.

function INDEX(FILE : **in** FILE_TYPE)
return POSITIVE_COUNT;   (359)

The function on line (360) returns the current size of the external file that is associated with the given file; it operates on a file of any mode.

function SIZE(FILE : **in** FILE_TYPE) **return** COUNT; (360)

The following function operates on a file of mode IN_FILE or INOUT_FILE. The function returns TRUE if the current index exceeds the size of the external file; otherwise the function returns false.

function END_OF FILE (FILE : **in** FILE_TYPE)
                                   return BOOLEAN;   (360.1)

10.2.3. The TEXT IO Package

The predefined TEXT_IO package provides facilities for input and output in a form readable by humans. Each file is read or written sequentially as a series of characters grouped into lines and as a sequence of lines grouped into pages.

The TEXT_IO package includes the facilities already described for SEQUENTIAL_IO and DIRECT_IO but with these differences:

- In place of READ, TEXT_IO uses a GET procedure.
- In place of WRITE, TEXT_IO uses a PUT procedure.

The GET and PUT procedures input values of suitable types from text files and output values to them.

In the TEXT_IO package, a text file consists of a sequence of lines, numbered from one. The characters in each line occupy consecutive character positions called *columns,* counted from one. Each character occupies a single column. A file may have a particular line length that is explicitly set by the user. If no line length is specified, lines may be any length up to the size of the file. The line length can be set or reset during execution of a program so that the same file can be written using both fixed line length—as for the production of tables—and variable line length—as during interactive dialogue. A file that is open has a current line number and a current column number. These determine the starting position available for the next GET or PUT operation.

10.2.3.1. Specification of line and page lengths.

The following subprograms provide for control of the line page structure of the TEXT_IO file. They provide for output of text with a specified maximum line length or page length. In all examples, the exception, STATUS_ERROR, is raised if the file to be used is not open.

procedure SET_LINE_LENGTH(FILE :
                    in FILE_TYPE; TO : **in** COUNT);   (361)
procedure SET_LINE_LENGTH(TO : **in** COUNT);   (362)

The procedures on lines (361) and (362) set the maximum line length of the specified output file to the number of characters specified by TO. The value zero for TO specifies an unbounded line length.

Page length is set by the following procedures:

> **procedure** SET_PAGE_LENGTH(FILE :
>   **in** FILE_TYPE; TO : **in** COUNT);   (363)
> **procedure** SET_PAGE_LENGTH(TO : **in** COUNT):   (364)

The maximum page length is set by the specified output file to the number of lines specified by TO. The value of zero for TO specifies an unbounded page length.

The currently set line length is returned by the following functions:

> **function** LINE_LENGTH(FILE : **in** FILE_TYPE)
>   **return** COUNT;   (365)
> **function** LINE_LENGTH **return** COUNT;   (366)

Lines (365) and (366) return the maximum line length currently set for the specified output file, or zero if the line length is unbounded.

> **function** PAGE_LENGTH(FILE : **in** FILE_TYPE)
>   **return** COUNT;   (367)
> **function** PAGE_LENGTH **return** COUNT;   (368)

Lines (367) and (368) return the maximum page length, or zero if the page length is unbounded.

10.2.3.2. Operations on columns, lines, and pages. The subprograms given in this section provide for explicit control of line and page structure; they operate either on the file given as the first parameter or, in the absence of the parameter, on the appropriate current default file. The exception, STATUS_ERROR, is raised by any of these subprograms if the file to be used in not open.

The following two procedures operate on a mode OUT_FILE.

> **procedure** NEW_LINE(FILE : **in** FILE_TYPE;
>   SPACING : **in** POSITIVE_COUNT := 1);   (369)
> **procedure** NEW_LINE(SPACING :
>   **in** POSITIVE_COUNT :=1);   (370)

The procedures output a line terminator and set the current column number to one, then increment the line number by one.

The SKIP_LINE procedures operate on a file of mode IN_FILE.

procedure SKIP_LINE(FILE : **in** FILE_TYPE;
       SPACING : **in** POSITIVE_COUNT := 1);   (371)
procedure SKIP_LINE(SPACING :
       in POSITIVE_COUNT := 1);   (372)

The procedures given in lines (371) and (372) reset the current column number to one and increment the current line number by SPACING.

The end-of-line boolean test is implemented by the functions given in lines (373) and (374) below.

function END_OF_LINE(FILE : **in** FILE_TYPE) **return**
       BOOLEAN;   (373)
function END_OF_LINE **return** BOOLEAN;   (374)

The end-of-line test operates on a file mode, IN_FILE. It returns TRUE if a line terminator or a file terminator is next; otherwise it returns FALSE.

The following procedures handle new pages.

procedure NEW_PAGE(FILE : **in** FILE_TYPE) ;   (375)
procedure NEW_PAGE;   (376)

Lines (375) and (376) operate on a file of mode OUT_FILE. The procedures output a line terminator if the current line is not terminated or if the current page is empty. The procedures then output a page terminator which terminates the current page, after which they add one to the current page number and set the current column and line numbers to one.

The end-of-page functions are given below.

function END_OF_PAGE(FILE : **in** FILE_TYPE) **return**
       BOOLEAN;   (377)
function END_OF_PAGE **return** BOOLEAN;   (378)

These functions operate on a mode of IN_FILE. The functions return TRUE if the combination of line terminator and page terminator or file terminator is next, otherwise FALSE.

The end-of-file boolean test is written in this manner:

function END_OF_FILE(FILE : **in** FILE_TYPE)
       return BOOLEAN;   (379)
function END_OF_FILE **return** BOOLEAN;   (380)

The above boolean tests operate on a file of mode IN_FILE. They return TRUE if a file terminator is next or if the combination of a line, a page, and a file terminator is next; otherwise they return a FALSE.

The following subprograms provide for the control of the current position of reading or writing in a file.

procedure SET_COL(FILE : **in** FILE_TYPE; TO : **in**
                                POSITIVE_COUNT);   (381)
procedure SET_COL(TO : **in** POSITIVE_COUNT);   (382)

The above procedures set the current column number to the value specified by TO. The current line number is unaffected.

function COL(FILE : **in** FILE_TYPE) **return**
                                POSITIVE_COUNT;   (383)
function COL **return** POSITIVE_COUNT;   (384)

The functions on lines (383) and (384) return the current column number.

The functions on lines (385) and (386) return the current line number.

function LINE(FILE : **in** FILE_TYPE) **return**
                                POSITIVE_COUNT;   (385)
function LINE **return** POSITIVE_COUNT;   (386)

The current page number is returned by the following functions:

function PAGE(FILE : **in** FILE_TYPE) **return**
                                POSITIVE_COUNT;   (387)
function PAGE **return** POSITIVE_COUNT;   (388)

10.2.4. Input-Output of Characters and Strings

The predefined GET and PUT procedures are used for both characters and strings. We will first discuss characters and then strings. The GET procedure is a form of the READ procedure. The PUT procedure is similar to the WRITE procedure.

procedure GET(FILE : **in** FILE_TYPE; ITEM : **out**
                                CHARACTER);   (389)
procedure GET(ITEM : **out** CHARACTER);   (390)

Line (389) defines ITEM as an out parameter of predefined type CHARACTER of the specified input file. The procedure on line (390) returns the character at the position given by the current line number and the current column number. It also adds one to the column number unless the line length is fixed and the current number equals the line length.

procedure PUT(FILE : **in** FILE_TYPE;
                ITEM : **in** CHARACTER);   (391)
procedure PUT(ITEM : **in** CHARACTER);   (392)

Lines (391) and (392) output the specified character to the specified output file on the current column of the current line. The procedures add one to the current column number unless the line length is fixed and the current number equals the line length.

When the ITEM type is a string, the length of the string is determined, after which the exact number of GET or PUT operations for the individual characters that comprise the string is carried out. To illustrate:

procedure GET(FILE : **in** FILE_TYPE; ITEM :
                    out STRING);   (393)
procedure GET(ITEM : **out** STRING);   (394)
procedure PUT(FILE : **in** FILE_TYPE; ITEM :
                    in STRING);   (395)
procedure PUT(ITEM : **in** STRING);   (396)

Note that lines (393) through (396) are very similar to lines (389) through (392).

Uniform generic procedures similar to the above are predefined for types other than CHARACTER and STRING, e.g., numeric, boolean, and enumeration. Analysis of each is beyond the scope of this text.

10.2.5. Low Level Input-Output

Low-level input-output provides direct control of peripheral devices. Control is implemented by two predefined procedures declared in the LOW_LEVEL_IO package. The two predefined procedures are (1) SEND_CONTROL and (2) RECEIVE_CONTROL.

The procedure SEND_CONTROL is used to send control information to a physical device. RECEIVE_CONTROL monitors the execution of an input-output operation by requesting information from the device. The two procedures have two parameters each that identify the physical device and the data. Inasmuch as the type of control information and the formats thereof depend on the physical and operational characteristics of the device, the parameters are implementation-defined. The specification of the package defining low-level IO is outlined as follows:

```
package LOW_LEVEL_IO is                            (397)
   -- declarations of the possible types for DEVICE and DATA
   -- declarations of overloaded procedures for these types
   procedure SEND_CONTROL   (DEVICE :
            device_type; DATA : in out data_type);   (398)
   procedure RECEIVE_CONTROL (DEVICE :
            device_type; DATA : in out data_type);   (399)
end;                                                 (400)
```

10.3. Example of Text Input-Output

Following is an example of text input-output. The example is a dialogue with a user at a terminal. The user is asked to select a color, and the program outputs the number of items of that color available in stock.

```
with TEXT_IO; use TEXT_IO;                         (401)
procedure DIALOGUE is                              (402)
   type COLOR is (WHITE, RED, ORANGE,
            YELLOW, GREEN, BLUE, BROWN);             (403)
   package COLOR_IO is new ENUMERATION_IO
            (ENUM => COLOR);                         (404)
   package NUMBER_IO is new INTEGER_IO
            (INTEGER);                               (405)
   use COLOR_IO, NUMBER_IO;                          (406)
   INVENTORY : array (COLOR) of INTEGER :=
            (20,17,43,10,28,173,87);                 (407)
   CHOICE : COLOR;                                   (408)
   procedure ENTER_COLOR (SELECTION :
            out COLOR) is                            (409)
      SELECTION : COLOR;                             (410)
   begin                                             (411)
      loop                                           (412)
```

```
begin                                                    (413)
  PUT ("Color selected: ");   - -   prompts user         (414)
  GET (SELECTION);   - -   accepts color typed
                            or raises exception           (415)
  exit;                                                  (415.1)
exception                                                (416)
  when DATA_ERROR =>                                     (417)
    PUT ("Invalid color, try again ");                   (418)
    NEW_LINE(2);                                         (419)
end;                                                     (420)
  end loop;                                              (421)
end;                                                     (422)
begin;   - -   statements of DIALOGUE                    (423)
  NUMBER_IO.DEFAULT_WIDTH := 5;                          (424)
  loop                                                   (425)
    ENTER_COLOR(CHOICE);   - -   User types color.       (426)
    NEW_LINE(2);                                         (426.1)
    SET_COL(5); PUT(CHOICE); PUT
                          ("Items Available: ");         (427)
PUT(INVENTORY(CHOICE));
    NEW_LINE;                                            (428)
  end loop;                                              (429)
end DIALOGUE;                                            (430)
```

In the actual operation of the above example, the user will see the following on the video screen:

Color selected: (431)

At this point, the user is prompted to select a color. Let us suppose he selects the color black. He types BLACK. The following will then appear on the screen:

Color selected: BLACK   (432)

The computer responds:

Invalid color, try again   (433)

As we already know, black is not one of the colors listed in line (403). When the user entered black, the exception handler, lines (416) through (419), took over and caused line (433) to appear on the user's screen. If the user now selects blue, the following will appear on the screen:

BLUE Items Available: 173   (434)

Chapter

11

Generics

11.0. Generics, General

Generic program units enable program modules to be written in a general form, then later, to be tailored to a particular need at the time of compilation. In other words, generic program units are templates of algorithms that may be customized for any number of applications that use the same fundamental algorithm. This permits the generalized module to be used again and again in the same program.

Inasmuch as generic modules are templates, they cannot be directly inserted in programs and executed as subprograms or packages. But by assigning parameters to generics, we are able to create independent subprogram and package modules that are executable program units. We call this process *generic instantiation*.

11.1. How To Create a Generic Program Module

Figure 11.1 illustrates the principal of how to create generic subprogram or package modules. The idea is to take a generalized subprogram or package unit and then add a prefix called the generic part. In concept the generic subprogram or package looks like Figure 11.1. To illustrate this concept, we will develop a specification for a generic stack package with push and pop features, after which we will show how to instantiate the package.

11.2. Development of an Example
Specification for a Generic Package

The *stack* is commonly conceived of as a data structure in which elements are stored by push operations and retrieved by pop operations. New elements are pushed, or stored, on the top level of the stack; elements already in the stack are pushed down one level. The *pop* operation retrieves the most recent element pushed onto the top of the stack. Thus information is retrieved on a last-in first-out basis.

Nongeneric stack structures require elements to be of a specific type, INTEGER, for example. In addition, the size, or capacity, of nongeneric stacks is fixed. The generic approach illustrated below allows us to define as many stacks as we wish, each with its own size and element type. Lines (435) through (442) are a generic specification for a package to formulate stacks.

generic	(435)
SIZE : POSITIVE;	(436)
type ITEM **is private**;	(437)
package STACK **is**	(438)
procedure PUSH (E : **in** ITEM);	(439)
procedure POP (E : **out** ITEM);	(440)
OVERFLOW, UNDERFLOW : **exception**;	(441)
end STACK;	(442)

Line (435) refers to the top-level box in Figure 11.1 labeled generic part. Lines (436) through (442) refer to the middle box in Figure 11.1, the area labeled generic specification. As previously stated, the generic specification is a template; it cannot be used directly in the program. To use the template, we instantiate it.

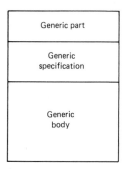

Figure 11.1 Concept of the generic subprogram or package.

11.3. How To Instantiate a Generic
Package Specification

We instantiate the generic specification by assigning values and types to the parameters. Referring back to lines (435) through (442), we can write:

package STACK_INT **is new** STACK(SIZE => 200,
                                            ITEM => INTEGER);   (443)

Line (443) creates an executable package called STACK_INT. This stack has a capacity of 200 items of type INTEGER.

Using the same generic, lines (435) through (442), we can create another executable program unit; it may look like this:

package STACK_BOOL **is new** STACK(100,
                                            BOOLEAN);   **(444)**

Line (444) creates a usable package called STACK_BOOL. This stack has a capacity of 100 elements of type BOOLEAN.

The packages STACK_INT and STACK_BOOL are both created from the generic package called STACK. Thus, we see that in the development of long programs the programmer has the opportunity of using the same generic over and over again. In this manner it is possible to create many different subprograms and packages that fundamentally use the same algorithm. This saves the programmer time and reduces programming errors. Inasmuch as packages STACK_INT and STACK_BOOL are created by instantiating the generic, we commonly refer to them as *instances* of the generic.

Note that after the example generic units, lines (443) and (444), have been instantiated at compilation time, there is no operational difference between the resulting program units—called instants— and program units that are individually written by a programmer. The procedures of the instantiated packages can be called as follows:

STACK_INT.PUSH(N);   (445)
STACK_BOOL.PUSH(TRUE);   (446)

11.4. Example of a Complete
Generic Package

The following program segment illustrates the formulation of the body of the generic package defined by the specification given in lines (435) through (442).

```
package body STACK is;                          (447)
   type TABLE is array (POSITIVE range <>)
                              of ITEM;           (448)
   SPACE : TABLE(1 . . SIZE);                    (449)
   INDEX : NATURAL := 0;                         (450)
   procedure PUSH(E : in ITEM) is                (451)
   begin                                         (452)
      if INDEX >= SIZE then                      (453)
         raise OVERFLOW;                         (454)
      end if;                                    (455)
      INDEX := INDEX + 1;                        (456)
      SPACE(INDEX) := E;                         (457)
   end PUSH;                                      (458)
   procedure POP(E : out ITEM) is                (459)
   begin                                         (460)
      if INDEX = 0 then                          (461)
         raise UNDERFLOW;                        (462)
      end if;                                    (463)
      E := SPACE(INDEX);                         (464)
      INDEX := INDEX-1;                          (465)
   end POP;                                       (466)
end STACK;                                        (467)
```

To use the complete generic package, we instantiate the module. As previously shown in line (443), we do this as follows:

```
package STACK_INT is new STACK(SIZE => 200,
                      ELEM => INTEGER);          (468)
```

Line (468) creates a usable package called STACK_INT. The stack size is stated as 200 items, and the elements are typed as INTEGER. We can call the package by the expression:

```
STACK_INT.PUSH(N);                               (469)
```

11.5. Summary Considerations Relating to Generics

As observed in the opening lines of this chapter, the primary purpose of generic units is to write segments of code which can be used many times. This is the same fundamental idea that underlies such common program constructs as loops.

Once written and tested, generic program units should be filed as library units and called as required. In this context, it should be noted that many of the predefined Ada language units commonly filed in libraries are actually generics. The predefined TEXT_IO and INPUT_OUTPUT packages are examples.

Part

2

Ada Program Development and Management

Chapters 2 through 11 covered the basics of developing and writing program modules in the Ada Language System. The fundamental Ada concepts of complete programs, subprograms, tasks, procedures, packages, input-output, and generic program units were studied. Techniques on how to write Ada program entities were presented.

At this point, we leave fundamentals and approach Ada as a language for both system design and application programming. We explain how to synthesize requirements and design operational systems, how to modularize the systems, and finally, how to write and test complete programs.

Chapter 12 presents Ada as both a design language and an application language. The chapter covers:

- Top-down system design
- Techniques to implement structured design procedures that modularize large programs
- How to use Ada as a system design language
- How to write Ada software for the modules developed in the previous two steps
- How to assemble Ada modules into an overall program
- Testing Ada software
- Establishing confidence in the reliability of software

In addition, Chapter 12 includes, as an example, a detailed discussion on how to design a packet message switch using Ada as a system design language. Then the chapter shows how to implement the design using Ada as an application language.

This chapter illustrates the impact of Ada on computer architecture. It shows how the synthesis of a system design using Ada as a design language will identify specific modules which may be implemented in either hardware or software. This forces engineers, system designers, and programmers to jointly determine which modules shall be hardware and which software.

In essence, the above approach to system architecture shows that in a well-designed system, the software must be designed first. This is a unique thought. In most situations, the hardware is designed virtually independently of software and ahead of software. In practice, this results in confusion, delayed operational dates, and overpriced software. The reasons for this situation are explained in Chapter 12.

Ada is an innovative system design and programming language. This means that the management of system designers, engineers, and programmers must in turn be innovative in addition to being effective. Chapter 13 is management-oriented. We explain new techniques to both organize and manage system design, development, and programming operations. We deal with specific points relating to the day-to-day management of technical personnel. Chapter 14 discusses the development of the Ada programming support environment (APSE). The APSE is also known as the Stoneman environment. Chapter 15 discusses Department of Defense implementation of the Ada Language System. The present status of Ada compiler development is included in this discussion. An important section of this chapter provides information on how to obtain Ada compilers.

12

How to Design, Construct, and Test Ada Programs

12.0. Introduction to Designing and Constructing Ada Programs

The Ada language was created for Department of Defense embedded computer systems. As noted in the introductory chapter, DOD considers embedded computers to be computers that are integral components of larger systems. Embedded computers vary in size from very small microcomputers—a computer on a single chip, for example—to the largest of the supercomputers. Program requirements also vary in size over a wide range from very small, as in the case of single-chip microcomputers, to very large, frequently containing hundreds of thousands of lines. Department of Defense embedded computers are expected to operate reliably, in field environments, and without the aid of programmers standing by. This operational philosophy applies to both very large and very small systems.

Acknowledging the above requirements, the developers of the Ada Language System worked on the basis that DOD and contractor personnel would develop, write, compile, and test software in central support facilities and then send to the field fully operational programs. In addition, the developers recognized that the computers in the central facilities are large systems that incorporate complete Ada compilers and have access to large program libraries. The computers in the support facilities have come to be known as *host computers;* those in the field are now called *target computers.*

The approach to programming for the environment described above is shown in Figure 12.1. This figure illustrates that the Ada approach to program design, coding, and testing is to develop and test the program on an existing host computer, then transfer the completed program to a target system—generally an embedded computer. However, the target may be a stand-alone system; it may even be the host. In other words, it is possible for the host and the target be the same system.

The developers of the Ada Language System also recognized that many DOD computer requirements start at the point where military operational requirements are synthesized into realizable technology. This is also the point where programming systems are conceived and design commences.

Using Ada as a design language, we are able to design complex programming systems for operational systems not yet built. We test the designs on an existing host computer. The host uses an Ada compiler. The compiler checks the validity of the system design. If the compilation process indicates a problem or an inconsistency in design, we modify the design, then test it again. This iterative technique permits us to design, test, then modify designs before the hardware is built and application programs are coded.

The above paragraphs mean that the program design features of the Ada language permit us to design and test workable software systems on an existing host computer before the hardware design of the target system is finalized. In practice, this methodology—software before hardware—substantially reduces costs.

Everyone agrees that computer software is complex. Some authorities argue that developing computer software is the most complex activity ever created by humanity. Large computer programs may be hundreds of thousands of lines long. Recognizing that the average page of text contains around fifty typed lines, single-spaced, it is obvious that a program in excess of 100,000 lines is very long indeed. It is also obvious that no one person or group of persons is capable

Figure 12.1 Transfer of programs from the host computer to the target computer.

of comprehending at one time all the details of developing such programs.

To understand and manage the development of complex programming systems, it is necessary that we divide these systems into smaller components or units that are both manageable and understandable. These units are called *modules*. It should be noted that some writers refer to Ada modules as compilation units. This book uses the term modules when referring to Ada program units, specifically, units that perform designated operations. Units are subprograms, procedures, tasks, packages, functions.

In concept, an Ada program is a collection of one or more modules submitted to a compiler in one or more operations. The modules may be specially written for a particular Ada program; they may be library modules that fit the application at hand; or they may be generic entities parameterized to fit the application. Individual modules are linked together in the compilation process on the host computer. The resulting product—a complete program—is transferred to the target system as Figure 12.1 illustrates.

In the design and development of large and complex systems, a number of programmers are assigned to the job. They work on individual modules, and they work in parallel with one another; they also work independently. Each must be able to develop and test his or her module without unnecessary dependence on other programmers. Management of programming activities is therefore very important. Personnel supervision is discussed in Chapter 13.

12.0.1. Organization of This Chapter

Section 12.1 shows how to use Ada both as a system design language and as an application programming language. Top-down structured programming principles are emphasized. The methodology to design Ada modules and integrate these modules into working programs is developed. In section 12.2 we present an example of how to use Ada, first as a design language in the synthesis of a packet message system, then as an application language in programming the system. Test and reliability are the subjects of the discussion in Section 12.3. This chapter touches on the management of programming activities. However, a more detailed discussion is presented in chapter 13.

12.1. System Design

In the development of any large DOD computer-based system, we first define the overall military operational requirements; then we systematically synthesize a system that fulfills the requirements. The synthesis utilizes a system design language. It is also an iterative process. In the final step, it establishes system architecture. Hardware and software components are determined, and the program design is finalized.

12.1.1. Definition of a System-Program Design Language

In the initial stages of system synthesis, the design language assists in developing the overall system architecture from which hardware and software designs are finalized. At this level, we define a *system design language* as a language for describing the control structure and general organization of a programming system. The system design language utilizes the Ada programming support environment (APSE) which includes the compiler. The APSE is discussed in detail in Chapter 14.

At this stage of the design procedure, the compiler does not generate code from system-program designs. In general, what the compiler does is analyze the syntax of statements, check for closure of structures, and perform type checking.

A system-program design language provides:

- An English language representation of the system-program operation that is easy to read and comprehend
- The ability to work in a top-down structured format that is capable of dividing large systems into manageable hardware and software modules
- A methodology to describe the functions of the system modules in readable English
- A syntax such that when the system program-design is written, it may be tested on a host computer using a compiler
- A medium for communication among engineers, the system designer, and programmers
- Step by step documentation for configuration management and periodic design reviews

Features of the Ada Language System provide facilities that fulfill the requirements listed above, and as a result, Ada is called a system-program design language. At the same time, Ada provides facilities for application programming; therefore, Ada is also known as a language for application programming.

The ability of Ada to handle both system-program design as well as application programming is unique. None of the existing popular languages provides the facilities needed for both design and application work. Fortran, Cobol, PL/1, and even Pascal, the newest of the popular languages, are application languages. They are not system design languages.

A number of companies have, through the years, developed programming techniques which they call design languages. These so-called languages cannot be run on a computer; they are therefore not design languages, but design methodologies. Still other companies have developed specialized program design languages that are run on a compiler. Many of these languages are excellent in the application for which they were designed. However, none have the syntactic richness of Ada. At this point, an example of Ada as a program design language is helpful.

12.1.2. Example of Ada as a Program Design Language

Lines (470) through (483)—a procedure for sorting a table—illustrate the use of Ada as a program design language.

```
procedure SORT (TABLE : in out TABLE_TYPE) is      (470)
    //declarations//;                              (471)
begin                                              (472)
    if //TABLE has more than one entry// then      (473)
        while //TABLE is not sorted// loop         (474)
            for //each pair of entries in TABLE// loop  (475)
                if //first entry is greater than second//  (476)
                then                               (477)
                    //exchange the two entries//;   (478)
                end if;                            (479)
            end loop;                              (480)
        end loop;                                  (481)
    end if;                                        (482)
end SORT;                                          (483)
```

In the above example, it will be noted that lines (470) and (471) are the specification; lines (472) through (483) comprise the body of the procedure. In both the specification and the body, a new technique for writing descriptive data is introduced. Specifically, information is enclosed by two sets of double slashes. This is because—taking lines (470) and (471) as examples—the compiler looks for a correct Ada statement on line (471) after processing line (470). The compiler will not accept a comment following two hyphens unless preceded by a legal Ada statement; in other words, the compiler would not accept:

```
procedure SORT (TABLE : in out TABLE_TYPE) is    (484)
-- declarations;                                   (485)
```

Comments written in the syntax of line (485) can only follow an Ada statement. The compiler will not accept line (485), but it will accept line (471). The text on line (471) looks like an Ada statement to the compiler. Implementation of the above design methodology requires that the APSE provide special software tools. This is explained in Chapter 14.

If the program design, lines (470) through (483), is run with the Ada compiler and no errors are discovered, we then go to the next step, which is to code the design. The exact code depends on the application; however, the following is a reasonable possibility:

```
procedure SORT (TABLE : in out TABLE_TYPE) is    (486)
   SWAPPED_ITEMS : boolean;                       (487)
   TEMP : ITEM_TYPE;                              (488)
begin                                             (489)
   if TABLE'LENGTH > 1 then                       (490)
      SWAPPED_ITEMS := TRUE;                      (491)
      -- loop while the table is not sorted       (492)
      while SWAPPED_ITEMS loop                    (493)
         SWAPPED_ITEMS := FALSE;                  (494)
         for I in TABLE'FIRST . . INDEX_TYPE'PRED
                            (TABLE'LAST)           (495)
         loop                                      (496)
            if TABLE(I) > table(INDEX_TYPE'SUCC(I)) (497)
            then                                   (498)
               SWAPPED_ITEMS := TRUE;             (499)
               TABLE (I) := TABLE(INDEX_TYPE'
                              SUCC(I));            (500)
```

```
                 TABLE (INDEX_TYPE'SUCC(I)) := TEMP;   (501)
            end if;                                     (502)
          end loop;    - -  for each pair of entries    (503)
        end loop;    - -  for sorting TABLE             (504)
      end if;                                           (505)
    end SORT;                                           (506)
```

Generic library modules are also used in program design. The
following specification for a package illustrates an Ada generic unit.

```
    generic                                             (507)
      type T is private;                                (508)
    package SEQUENCE is                                 (509)
      procedure NEXT (X : out T);                       (510)
      procedure CURRENT (X : out T);                    (511)
      procedure RESET;                                  (512)
      procedure EMPTY;                                  (513)
      function IS_EMPTY return BOOLEAN;                 (514)
      //other statements//;                             (515)
    end SEQUENCE;                                       (516)
```

The validity of the above specification can be proven on an Ada
compiler.

The reader may question the correctness of writing comments
on line (492) of the previous example and line (515) of the generic.
The technique is valid and will be accepted by the compiler because
in each case the comment follows a complete and correct Ada statement on the preceding line.

12.1.3. Basic Design Methodology

A workable system-program design language is best implemented
by a design methodology that, by utilizing a top-down stepwise re-
finement technique, divides large program structures into smaller

Figure 12.2 How to subdivide an algorithm into smaller units.

units, then links the units into an overall program. A simple example illustrates the principle. Consider the problem illustrated by Figure 12.2, a program tree that subdivides the overall problem—sorting a list of names—into three smaller units. The root of the tree is the statement of the problem. In the first move we divide the tree into three branches called *nodes*. At each of the three nodes, we write an English language statement that says what is to be done. We next move down each branch, replacing the English language statement of what is to be done with an algorithm for doing it. We continue this process until we have reached an elemental process that cannot be further subdivided.

The process described above is formalized in the design discipline commonly called *top-down structured programming*.

The program segments that top-down structured programming techniques create are called modules. We will next consider the Ada concept of modules, then show the tie-in to the structured programming discipline.

12.1.4. The Ada Concept of Modules

In general terms and as noted previously in this text, an Ada program module is an independent program entity that performs specific operations. Inasmuch as Ada modules are independent entities, they are similar in concept to manufactured piece parts. For example, an automobile part is manufactured independently of the rest of the car. When correctly installed in the vehicle, it works. In theory, the same holds true of Ada modules. They are designed and coded independently of the rest of the system. When inserted in the existing system, they work.

For the above theory to hold true in the real world, it is necessary that designers divide systems into unique modules that perform well-defined tasks. The ideal module performs only one operation and cannot be further subdivided. This means that programs must be subdivided into the smallest practical segments. The next section shows how to modularize systems.

12.1.5. How To Modularize System Designs

We modularize large system designs by utilizing a top-down methodology. As previously explained, top-down is a design technique that goes from the big picture to the small. In other words, going from a general idea to an elaborate and detailed system consisting of a configuration of simple interconnected modules.

The decomposition procedure is a consistent stepwise movement through rigorous, well-planned stages. In each stage we subdivide actions until the process terminates in elemental operations that cannot reasonably be further subdivided. Figure 12.3 illustrates top-down methodology and modularization concepts. It is a hypothetical system illustrating the relationships among the modules of a major task. Each box represents a module. Level 1 in Figure 12.3 defines what is to done; we call this level module A. Module A subdivides into three subtasks, modules B, C, and D on level 2. Module B reduces to module E on level 3. This module cannot be further subdivided. Module C on level 2 is subdivided into two modules, F and G, on level 4. These modules cannot be further subdivided. Module D on level 2 is not further reduced.

To develop Figure 12.3, we followed these steps:

- Defined a major operational requirement.

- Defined the requirement, called it module A, and placed it on level 1 in the program tree.

- Subdivided module A into three subtasks, modules B, C, and D, and placed these modules on level 2.

- Defined module E, level 3, a subdivision of module B.

- Examined module E and found that it could not be further subdivided.

- Subdivided module C into modules F and G and placed these modules on level 4; we skipped level 3 in this specific chain to

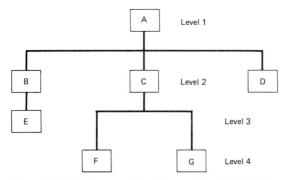

Figure 12.3 Top-down methodology and modularization concepts.

simplify graphics. On examining modules F and G, we found they could not be further subdivided.

- Examined module D and found that it could not be further subdivided.

From a system operational standpoint, we can make these comments concerning Figure 12.3.

- Module A on level 1 controls modules B, C, and D on level 2.
- Module B, level 2, controls module E on level 3.
- Module C controls modules F and G on level 4.

How to develop program trees using the principles of top-down structured programming applicable to the Ada language is explained in Section 12.1.5.1.

12.1.5.1. Developing program trees using top-down structured programming.

We have already noted that the expression top-down means going from the big picture to the small. However, the term structured programming involves additional concepts.

Structured programming is a design discipline. Its principles are applicable at any level of programming. They are particularly useful with design languages, especially design languages that are also application languages. The basic premise of structured programming is that by rigorous mathematical treatment—the details of which are beyond the scope of this text—we can show that any algorithm capable of being flowcharted may be represented by combinations of basic program control structures. Control structures are covered in detail in Chapter 4.

An *algorithm,* by definition and as used in this text, is an English language statement of a problem or a process. Commonly, it is a concise mathematical statement of a problem to be solved. The algorithm is written to be read and understood by people. It cannot be understood by the computer. Translating the algorithm to computer language is programming. And as previously stated, any algorithm that can be flowcharted can be represented by combinations of the basic control structures.

Classic top-down structured programs use the following basic structures:

- A linear sequence of operations.
- An *either-or* statement, which may also be construed as an *if-then-else* statement.

- A *do-until* statement. Variations on the *do until* are the *do-while* and the *case* statements.

The basic rules of top-down structured design are rigid; they are:

- In a system-program tree, control flows from the top down. In other words, modules on the higher level control modules on the next lower level.

- Each module has one entry and one exit; modules do not communicate with each other on a horizontal level.

- Data flow up or down.

- The common **goto** command is not used.

- Flow charts are not used.

12.1.5.2. How to develop system-programs designs using the program tree. The fundamental procedure is this: We first develop the program tree; then we design the program working from the top down. We consider each box to be a module.

Using Figure 12.3 as an example, we conceive of module A on level 1 as a primitive computer controlling a black box that contains modules B, C, D, E, F, and G. We determine the control functions performed by module A, then we design the program module for these functions. Next we test the code, using a program stub that represents the theoretical black box controlled by module A. The programmer who codes module A must also develop and code the program stub.

In the same manner, we design the three modules on level 2 and individually test each module. Next we design and test level 3. And finally, we design and test modules F and G on level 4. When the modules have been designed and tested, the program is linked together. Figure 12.3 is a program tree comprising seven Ada modules. The next section will discuss how to link these modules.

12.1.6. How To Link Ada Modules

As pointed out in previous chapters, Ada program entities or modules, consist of two parts, the specification and the body, or action part. The specification is the module's interface to the outside world. Users cannot access the body of an Ada module; they access only the specification. This means that the link between or among modules is the specification. To illustrate, consider Figure 12.4, actually a reprint of the first two levels of Figure 12.3.

Figure 12.4 will be developed as a package containing a group of procedures. Module A is a package; modules B, C, and D are procedures. The specifications of the four modules A, B, C, and D link the units. Module A issues calls as required to modules B, C, or D. The calls to modules B, C, and D are in the body of module A. The calls are directed to the specifications of modules B, C, or D. In this manner the interfaces of modules A, B, C, and D are automatically established.

In outline form, the program design for the example specification looks like this:

```
package MODULE_A is                              (517)
  //declarations//;                              (518)
  procedure MODULE_B;                            (519)
  procedure MODULE_C;                            (520)
  procedure MODULE_D;                            (521)
  //other declarations//;                        (522)
end MODULE_A;                                    (523)
```

The action part of package MODULE_A that calls the three procedures is written in this manner:

```
package body MODULE_A is                         (524)
begin                                            (525)
  //local declarations//;                        (526)
  case X is                                      (527)
    when 1 => procedure MODULE_B;                (528)
    when 2 => procedure MODULE_C;                (529)
    when others => procedure MODULE_D;           (530)
  end case;                                      (531)
end MODULE_A;                                    (532)
```

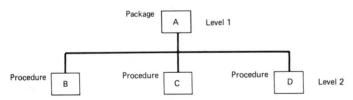

Figure 12.4 How to nest a group of procedures within a package.

Lines (524) through (532) say that when a variable in MOD-ULE_A—call the variable X—is equal to 1, then MODULE_B is called. When X is equal to 2, MODULE_C is called. When X equals anything else, MODULE_D is called. The preceding example shows how to take three independent procedures and link them into a program.

12.2. Example of System Design

The following discussion develops the fundamental system design of a packet message switch. Prior to the actual switch design, packet and circuit concepts are discussed. The packet message switch designed in this section is similar to many now in use in contemporary commercial networks. Section 12.2.1 below explains packet message systems. Readers should read and understand this section before proceeding to the actual design sections.

12.2.1. Explanation of a Packet Message System

In packet message systems, individual messages—teletype messages are a familiar example—are subdivided into individual units that do not exceed a fixed number of characters. These units are called *packets*. In the case of the world's first packet common carrier—the Department of Defense ARPANET, also known as the DAR-PANET—the maximum packet length was originally set at 1096 bits. That equates to 137 eight-bit ASCII characters. Using this criterion, the ARPANET designers defined a packet as a message not exceeding 1096 bits.

In the real world, the length of most messages exceeds 137 characters. This is not a problem to the packet communication system. In packet systems, there is a computer at each node. These computers subdivide messages that exceed 137 characters into standard length packets, i.e., 1096 bits maximum. For example, if a message is, say, 400 characters long, it is divided into three packets; the first and second packets are 137 characters each, the third is 126 characters. Packets are numbered for identification and then forwarded over the network. The node computer at the message destination reassembles the packets into the original message.

Figure 12.5 illustrates three nodes of a packet network. Information is shown going in one direction only, i.e., from node 1 to node 2, node 2 to node 3, then to an undefined node. Obviously, for a packet to go from node 3 to node 1, the packet must go around a circle that will eventually return it to node 1. We call this configuration a *circular network;* it's a common form of packet message system. The circular network can also be designed for two-way communication, i.e., node 2 to node 3, or alternatively, node 3 to node 2. This technique increases reliability; it provides two routes to each node.

For convenience in this discussion, let us assume one-way transmission as shown in Figure 12.5. Here is what happens in a packet network:

1. Looking at Figure 12.5, the network delivers a packet at node 1.

2. The switching computer at this node examines the packet, reads the address, and asks the question: Is the packet for this node or for another?

3. If the answer is this node, the node 1 computer collects all the packets that comprise the message as they arrive, then reassembles the message in its original form, after which it forwards the message to the local addressee.

4. If the answer to the question asked in 2 is no, the node 1 computer forwards the packet to node 2 where the same procedure is followed.

5. Messages may be originated at local terminals that communicate with the nodes. These messages enter the nodes via the local input circuits shown in Figure 12.5. The node computers packet the messages and forward the packets down the line.

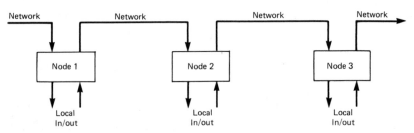

Figure 12.5 Basic packet message system.

An identical procedure is followed at each node.

Before proceeding with the design of the node switching computer, we must first be certain that we fully understand the basic circuit concepts upon which a packet message switch is built. These concepts are explained in the next section.

12.2.2. Fundamental Circuit Concepts

Figures 12.6*a*, *b*, and *c* illustrate three fundamental circuit concepts necessary to a full understanding of modern packet communication systems. Looking at these figures, we note the following:

- Figure 12.6*a* illustrates the principle of message concentration. The sketch shows three channels, A, B, and C, providing input to module D. In module D, messages arriving from the three channels are packetized and then forwarded to the next node over channel E. The messages may be forwarded in the sequence in which they arrive in module D, or they may be sent by preestablished priority. Figure 12.6*a* is sometimes called a *fan-in operation*.

- Figure 12.6*b* illustrates the principle of message deconcentration. In this sketch messages arrive over channel E in serial sequence. They are sorted by module F and forwarded to their respective

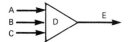

Figure 12.6*a*   Message concentrator.

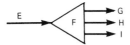

Figure 12.6*b*   Message deconcentrator.

Figure 12.6*c*   Communication system incorporating the message concentrator and the message deconcentrator.

destinations over channels G, H, and I. Packets are forwarded in their arrival sequence or according to preestablished priority.

- Figure 12.6c shows module D and module F interconnected to form a complete communication system.

Note the following points:

- Messages arrive at module D on a random basis. In other words, three messages may arrive at module D simultaneously.

- Module D packetizes messages and forwards them over channel E serially in the order of their arrival or according to preestablished priority.

- Module F accepts incoming message packets in serial sequence, sorts them by address, and forwards them to their destination in their arrival order, which is also their order of priority. Recall that module D forwarded message packets by priority.

Consideration of Figure 12.6a, b, and c reveals the fact that the system performs time-division multiplexing without the need of synchronization between the transmitting and receiving terminals. In practice this means:

- An increase in system capacity
- Higher speed
- Lower equipment cost
- Lower operating costs
- Lower maintenance costs

12.2.3. Functional Principles of a Node Switch in a Packet Network

Figures 12.7a and 12.7b illustrate the functional principles of a node switch in a packet network.

Figure 12.7a is identical in concept to the node switches illustrated in the network segment shown in Figure 12.5. Looking at Figure 12.7a, we note:

- Messages arriving at the node from the network are labeled PCKT_IN.

- Messages addressed to the node are forwarded to the local network via the output port called LOCAL_IN which fans them out to local addressees.

- Messages that arrive in the node from the network and are destined for another address are forwarded to the next node in the network over the outgoing channel labeled PCKT_OUT.

- Locally originated messages enter the node via the channel labeled LOCAL_OUT. These messages are transmitted to the next node in the network via the PCKT_OUT channel.

The node switch does not follow a set sequence of operations. To illustrate, the switch may be at rest; then a message for another node may arrive at the LOCAL_OUT port. At the same time, a packet from the network may arrive at the PCKT_IN port. In other words, the switch must perform any switching operation in a random sequence, and frequently, the switch may be required to perform two or more operations simultaneously.

At this point we draw a functional diagram of what goes on in the node switch. Figure 12.7b is such a functional diagram. In Figure

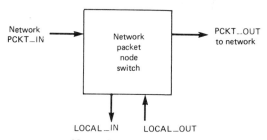

Figure 12.7a   Network packet node switch, input, output.

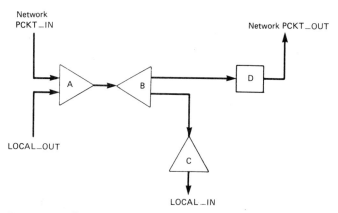

Figure 12.7b   Functional diagram of the network packet node switch.

12.7*b*, units A, B, C, and D are separate modules. The line marked PCKT_IN represents the incoming packet channel. The line marked PCKT_OUT represents the outgoing packet channel. This line goes to the next node switch.

Module A accepts packets as they arrive over the network in serial format and in a sequence established by their respective priorities at the previous node. Module A also accepts locally originated messages which it packetizes. If module A is processing a network packet at the same moment that it is handling a locally originated packet, the module compares the priorities of the two packets. On the basis of this comparison, packets are forwarded to module B in serial sequence and in the order of their individual priorities. Module B reads the address of each packet. If the address is this node, the packet is forwarded to module C. Module C collects the incoming packets, reassembles messages, and distributes them to local addressees in a fan-out operation. If module B determines that the packet address is another node in the network, the packet is forwarded to module D from which point it is sent to the next node. All four modules may be required to perform several functions simultaneously.

Obviously, operations such as those described in the above paragraphs cannot be programmed using flowcharts. The sequence of operations is random, and the operations are complex.

Some important points to remember from this section are:

1. The switch automatically performs an efficient asynchronous time-division multiplexing operation.
2. As noted on several occasions within this chapter, the sequence of operations within the switch is random.
3. Within each packet switch, a number of operations may occur simultaneously.
4. Packet switches may be programmed to process messages by priority.

The next section explains how to design the node switch and handle operational situations such as those described above.

12.2.4. Design of the Node Switch

The Ada Language System is designed to cope with operational problems such as those described in the above section. The problems are approached using top-down structured technology. Figure 12.8 illustrates.

This figure shows an Ada package with four procedures. They correspond by letter designation to the four modules in Figure 12.7b. An outline specification for the package shown in Figure 12.8 that implements the functional diagram shown in Figure 12.7b is given below.

package SWITCH **is**	(533)
//type declarations//;	(534)
procedure module_A;	(535)
procedure module_B;	(536)
procedure module_C;	(537)
procedure module_D;	(538)
//additional declarations//;	(539)
end SWITCH;	(540)

Lines (533) through (540) comprise an outline Ada package specification for the functional diagram shown in Figure 12.7b and further

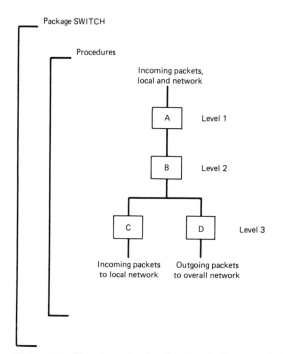

Figure 12.8 How to make the functional diagram of the packet node. Switch into a top-down structured program tree using Ada concepts.

developed by the program tree in Figure 12.8. As previously noted, the overall specification is a package. It includes four principal procedures.

At this point, the system designers will test the specification on a host computer equipped with an Ada compiler. If the specification compiles correctly, the system designers—programmers and engineers—determine which modules will be realized in hardware and which in software. When this determination is made, programmers start writing the code for the bodies of the individual tasks. This is application programming.

From the above, it will be noted that the transition from system design to application programming is not a clear line; rather, it is a gradual movement from a generalized system description to specific application programming.

Modules A, B, C, and D are very similar. Therefore, this is a good application for generic program design units. The alert designer will first develop a generic module representative of modules A, B, C, and D. This will be filed as a library unit. As required, it can be called by the programmers, formalized by specific parameters, then used at each node in the system. This reduces the overall programming effort. As a result, accuracy is improved and costs decrease.

12.2.5. Impact on Computer Architecture

In the previous discussion, we said that if the specification compiles correctly, the system designers—programmers and engineers—determine which modules will be realized in hardware and which in software. This approach is a radical innovation, directly impacting both hardware and software design. It forces engineers and programmers to work together.

12.3. System Test and Reliability

Much has been written in books and in technical papers on software test, validation, reliability, quality control, etc. Generally speaking, the material is worthless. The problem is that most writers try to apply hardware quality-control practices to software. This does not work. Hardware is subject to wear; eventually it breaks down. Computer software never wears out. Remember, a computer program is simply a series of instructions that tell a computer what to do and in what sequence. The program does not wear out as a result of usage.

The following sections explain how to test and validate Ada programs—or for that matter, programs written in other languages—and as a result how to develop confidence in the programs.

12.3.1. Basic Techniques

Program validation begins the moment pencil is first put to paper. For accurate programming, a programmer must use a disciplined, stylized approach. Consider, for example, the following segment of code, actually a repeat of lines (130) through (152).

```
type VECTOR is array (INDEX range <>)
                       of INTEGER;        (541)
type INDEX is range 1 . . 500;            (542)
procedure SORT (A : in out VECTOR) is     (543)
   J : INDEX;                             (544)
   TEMP : INTEGER;                        (545)

begin                                     (546)
   for                                    (547)
      I in A'FIRST . . A'LAST             (548)
   loop                                   (549)
      J := I;                             (550)
      while                               (551)
         J < A'LAST                       (552)
      loop                                (553)
         J := J+1;                        (554)
         if                               (555)
            A(I) > A(J);                  (556)
         then                             (557)
            TEMP := A(I);                 (558)
            A(I) := A(J);                 (559)
            A(J) := TEMP;                 (560)
         end if;                          (561)
      end loop;                           (562)
   end loop;                              (563)
end SORT;                                 (564)
```

Lines (541) through (564) illustrate a stylized graphical approach to the writing of computer code. Note that every segment of the program is indented under an appropriate heading, and in addition, lines are skipped between segments. Thus:

- In the specification portion, all items under the title, **procedure SORT**, are indented three spaces. At the end of the specification, a line is skipped.

- The body commences on line (546). Every operation or statement in the body is also indented under its control word. This technique clarifies nesting and permits the programmer to rapidly check by eye the correctness of each operation under each control word.

- The technique permits us to check for an **end** control word whenever a particular construct requires it. Thus the **loop** on line (553) requires an **end** statement; this appears on line (562) as **end loop**. The major loop that begins on line (549) ends on line (563) with another **end loop**.

Experience shows that the stylized graphics technique outlined above reduces programming errors because:

- Programmers catch human errors by reading the program.

- It is easy for a programmer to see that only correct operations are listed under each control word.

- Programmers recently assigned to the job will quickly come up to speed.

The reader will, of course, note that the technique described above has been consistently followed throughout this book.

12.3.2. How To Test Programs

In earlier sections of this chapter, we discussed top-down structured design techniques. This approach stresses hierarchical decomposition of operational requirements into definable modules. In this context, consider Figure 12.9, a reprint of Figure 12.3. We have already said that in the top-down decomposition of a system we first define module A. Next, we define the level 2 modules, after which we define those on levels 3 and 4. We have also said that module A may be thought of as a primitive computer controlling a black box that comprises the rest of the program. Likewise, we consider module B as a primitive computer controlling another black box, module E. Module C is the primitive device that controls the black box comprising modules F and G.

To test the system design, we first write the specification for module A. Next, we test it on a host computer using an Ada compiler. This test tells us of any syntactic errors that may be in the specification. Next we define modules B, C, and D, and we write separate specifications for each of the three modules. We check these specifications on the host machine. We proceed through the entire program design in this manner.

We already know that the software for each module comprises two major sections, specification and body. We also know that in the body of module A, we can write a **case** command that will call modules B, C, or D, thus establishing the interfaces with module A on level 1 and any of the three modules on level 2. In the case of module B, a call in the body of the module B program will call module E. This automatically establishes the interface between modules B and E. Relative to module C, a **case** command in the module C program body will call either module F or module G. As before, the interfaces are automatically established.

When we write the program for the body of module A, we will include provisions for calling modules B, C, and D as required. To test module A, we must make provisions for something to happen when the body, or action portion, of module A selects one of the three modules—B, C, or D—on the basis of the **case** command. To do this, we can either write program stubs, or to be more practical, we can provide the actual specifications of modules B, C, or D, assuming we have already written the specifications and checked their syntax.

Note that once we have written the code for both the specification and the body of module A on level 1, all that is needed to check

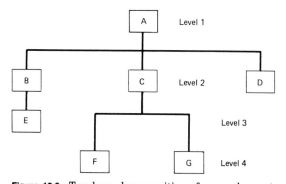

Figure 12.9 Top-down decomposition of a complex system into a program tree.

the interface of module A with any module on level 2 is to write the specification for the level 2 modules. At this point, we do not need to write bodies for the modules on level 2. Another important point to note is this: When the modules for each level are coded in a program, the interfaces between modules are automatically tested each time the system is exercised.

In summary, the procedure for testing and validating programs is this:

1. In a step-by-step decomposition process, we modularize systems, then we design and test the specifications for each level of the program tree.

2. Following step one, we develop programs for the bodies of each module.

3. We check the syntax of the programs for the module bodies using the Ada compiler on the host machine; then we exercise the system top down.

Recognize this point: None of the modules below level 1 can operate without control signals and data provided by module A on the top level. This feature directly impacts system testing. For example, consider module E on level 4. Assume we have completed coding that module and wish to test it. We do not need to write a program stub for module E, because it is the last one in the chain. However, to test module E, we also must exercise both modules A and B. In other words, in testing module G, we exercise a chain of modules, A, B, and E. Figure 12.10 —actually the left-hand side of Figure 12.9—illustrates:

In testing modules F or G, we actually test modules A, C, and F or modules A, C, and G as shown in Figure 12.11, the mid-section

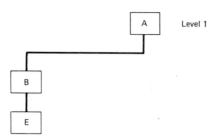

Figure 12.10 Top-down dynamic testing of modules A, B, E.

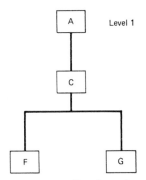

Figure 12.11 Top-down dynamic testing of modules A, C, F and modules A, C, G.

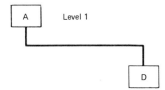

Figure 12.12 Top-down dynamic testing of modules A and D.

of Figure 12.9. In testing module D, we test modules A and D together as illustrated by Figure 12.12, the right-hand side of Figure
12.9. The above procedure shows that the highest level modules
in the program tree are the most tested. This is advantageous because it prevents system-wide errors. Module test and system test
is further discussed in Chapter 13, "Management," section 13.7.

12.3.3. Summary of Testing

Software testing—frequently called *validation*—may be broken into
two general categories, static analysis and dynamic testing.

12.3.3.1. Static analysis. The term *static analysis* refers to desk check-
ing segments of code. It is not truly testing but is a program validation technique. The goal is to discover heretofore unnoticed flaws,
such as logic and coding errors, all of which cause difficulties in
dynamic testing.

Static analysis is a continuing process; it starts when the programmer writes the first line of code. It is aided by the discipline of
top-down structured design and the various graphical techniques

presented throughout this book, such as line indentation, use of underlining, capital letters, various graphical methods for showing structures. It is also implemented by walk-throughs such as those described in the next chapter.

Ada substantially reduces the labor of static analysis in the following sense. We have already pointed out that Ada program modules are independent entities linked via their specifications. The configuration management tools provided as part of the Ada programming support environment automatically maintain a record of module interfaces as defined by their specifications and automatically check their compatibility.

12.3.3.2. Dynamic testing. Dynamic testing, performed on a computer, divides into two principal categories, module and system testing. Ideally, dynamic testing should occur in a live environment with actual input stimulus. From a practical standpoint, this is usually impossible. Therefore, program drivers and stubs representing modules which interface with the unit under test must be generated.

Module testing exercises a module through its full range of inputs and outputs. In this context, the module must be conceived of as a black box with one input and one output. Input data and control commands are forwarded to the module. The module output over its entire range is evaluated against written requirements and standards. If corrections or changes are necessary, they should be made immediately; then the module is again tested.

Dynamic system testing proves that the overall system performs in a manner compatible with operational requirements and specifications. It begins as soon as testing begins with the top module in the program tree hierarchy, level 1 in Figures 12.10, 12.11, and 12.12. When the test of the level 1 module determines the design to be correct and the unit to be correctly programmed, the modules on the next lower level are tested as shown in Figures 12.10, 12.11, and 12.12. Thus, by incremental growth, subordinate modules are tested, then integrated into a system of previously tested modules. When all the modules have been integrated into an overall system and tested, a working and reliable software product results.

13

Management

13.0. The Football Coach

To successfully handle Ada programming operations and realize the benefits of the language, effective management of system design, program design, and application programming is essential.

The dictionary defines management as "the act, manner, or practice of managing, handling, directing, or controlling." This definition is incomplete. Management is also an exercise in the dynamics of power and authority. In practice, it is an acquired art; it includes all the many facets of human relations, especially the ability to motivate others to work and perform beyond their perceived limits. In addition, the manager must develop a dynamic esprit de corps among his or her employees. In effect, the successful Ada programming manager is like a good football coach who motivates players to work hard, to perform beyond their perceived capabilities, to be fiercely loyal, and at the same time, to be good team players that work together to win. This chapter tells how to manage Ada programming operations.

A discussion of how to motivate programmers and measure their performance is included.

13.1. Attributes of the Manager

There are many different ways to manage. Each manager has a particular style. Nevertheless, certain attributes are common to all management techniques. For managing large system development and programming projects in the Ada language, the fundamental attributes successful managers show are:

- The ability to understand user requirements and translate them into meaningful technology
- A thorough understanding of system operations—both hardware and software
- An overall understanding of the Ada language and the ability to design and code programs
- The ability to both motivate personnel and command loyalty

The manager described above is an experienced "hands-on" type.

The successful manager exhibits other specialized attributes in addition to those listed. These will be discussed at different points in the balance of this chapter. The best manager does not perform well unless supported by a well-defined, functioning organization. Accordingly, the next section of this chapter discusses organization.

13.2. Organization

The manager charged with creating and running an organization to perform system design, program design, and application programming—all in the Ada language—directly controls:

- System design, program design, and application programming
- Configuration management
- System test

In addition to the above functions, the manager maintains a close liaison with engineering.

These managerial functions are keyed to the development stages of a project. However, once the system is developed, tested, and deployed in an operational environment, the manager still retains a responsibility—one generally called postdeployment support, or sometimes, system maintenance.

In the postdeployment period the Ada project manager has a continuing responsibility because:

- User operational requirements change
- Software requirements change
- Hardware design evolves

In other words, we recognize that every operational system is subject to change. Therefore, the effective manager is one who can be flexible as the occasion demands. Changes that result from modified operational requirements almost always generate software modifications. Modified hardware requirements may or may not change software.

Chapter 12 points out that Department of Defense embedded computers are expected to operate reliably, in field environments, and without the aid of programmers standing by. DOD personnel and supporting contractors are expected to develop, write, compile, and test programs in a central support facility using a host computer. The finalized program is then sent to the field where it is implemented on an operating computer called the target system. If user operational requirements change, the manager in the central support facility is responsible for implementing necessary program changes. Figure 13.1 outlines an organizational approach that handles the requirements of both the system development and the post-deployment periods.

Figure 13.1 shows three major functions reporting directly to the project manager. It also shows that the manager maintains an interface with the user and a liaison with his or her own engineering organization. To effectively manage a large Ada system design and

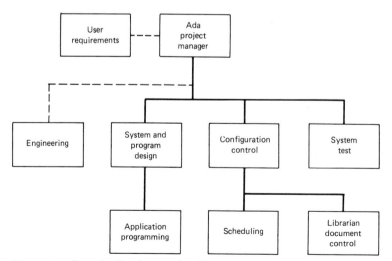

Figure 13.1 Organization for a major Ada programming project.

programming effort, the manager must possess the attributes previously listed; and in addition, must:

- Know how to maintain firm control of both the overall system configuration and the subsystem configurations
- Run rigid and comprehensive operational tests on both the unit and system levels

Studies in management psychology show that if too many key personnel report directly to a manager, that manager tends to lose control. The best managers do not have more than six or seven unit managers reporting directly to them. In the organization outlined in Figure 13.1, three unit managers report to the project manager. The top level of Figure 13.1 shows the project manager as the interface between the user's operational requirements and the overall project. This is important. If the user has direct access to any of the three divisions, those divisions will receive instructions from two sources, the manager and the user. The manager will soon lose control. The customer will think he is not getting through to the programmers. The result will be chaos.

The Ada project manager must also maintain a close working relationship with hardware design engineers. The effective project manager knows where the project is going; i.e., he knows the schedule, what each division is doing, what technical problems are occurring and why. The effective manager also knows what to expect from his or her personnel and is alert to personnel problems.

To accomplish all of the aforesaid, the manager utilizes five simple, but very effective management tools:

1. The bar chart
2. The circle chart
3. The program tree
4. The HIPO diagram
5. The structured walk-through

In addition, he uses strong personnel management techniques. These will be discussed in section 13.8 of this chapter. The first management tool that will be analyzed is the bar chart.

13.3. The Bar Chart

Figure 13.2 illustrates a hypothetical bar chart, representing a group of horizontal lines plotted against time. Each line represents a module, a part of an overall project. The chart is read from left to right. The start date of each subtask is read from the left side of the chart; the completion date is read on the right. As an example, module 3 is read as starting in the middle of the second month of the project and is scheduled for completion just after the start of the tenth month.

Bar chart scheduling is common in manufacturing industries, especially the long established "smokestack" factories such as automobile plants. In these industries, it is a reasonably accurate planning technique because production line manufacturing methods are long established; potential problems are well known.

The bar chart alone is not recommended for planning innovative research and development projects or large computer software efforts. The difficulty is that the chart does not show relationships between modules. In other words, an objective observer cannot study the chart and know which modules are dependent on which. In smokestack industries, this is not a problem, because experienced production engineers intuitively know the task relationships and dependencies.

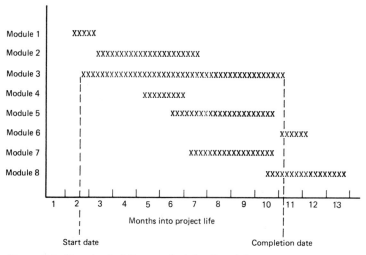

Figure 13.2 Bar chart, delivery schedule of modules.

When the bar chart is combined with a circle chart and a program tree, meaningful scheduling results. The effect of reading the three charts together is synergistic. The circle chart is discussed in the next section. Figure 13.3 illustrates the principle of the circle chart.

13.4. The Circle Chart

Figure 13.3 shows, by means of interconnected circles, the relationships of the eight modules in the Ada design and programming project represented by the bar chart, Figure 13.2. Each circle represents an Ada module, i.e., a package or a subprogram. The fundamental theory of the circle chart is that in showing the relationship between modules, the chart identifies the input that each module requires before it can be completed. The chart is read from left to right. Using Figure 13.3 as an example, we learn that:

- Module 1, represented by circle 1, must be complete before modules 2 and 3 are complete.

- Module 4 requires input from modules 2 and 3 before it is complete.

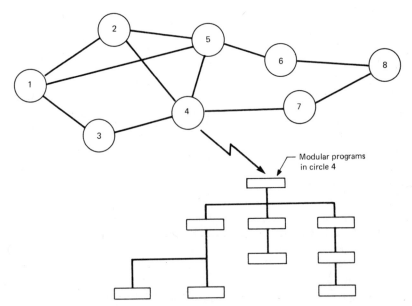

Figure 13.3 Circle chart, relationship of major modules.

- Module 5 requires input from modules 1, 2, and 4 before it is complete.
- Modules 6 and 7 require input from modules 5 and 4 respectively.
- Module 8, the last module to be completed, requires input from modules 6 and 7.

Within each module, both program design and application programming are accomplished. For example, module 4 may be a package represented by the program tree connected with circle 4 in Figure 13.2.

To reiterate the point already made, the circle chart shows the relationships among the modules of a major programming effort. In showing relationships, the chart points to possible sources of delay. For example, if there is a delay in work on, say, module 2, the manager immediately knows that module 4 may be delayed and can plan accordingly. This cannot be known with only a bar chart.

The reader may regard the circle chart as a form of PERT scheduling. Such an outlook is a misconception. PERT is a scheduling technique. The circle chart does not schedule anything. It shows relationships among modules.

13.5. Summary of Scheduling

The bar chart in Figure 13.2, shows the start and end dates for work on the various modules of a major project. The circle chart, Figure 13.3, shows the relationships of the modules, i.e., the input each module requires before it can be completed. The program tree that accompanies each module—circle in Figure 13.3—graphically shows the work that must be performed in each module.

For scheduling to be effective, i.e., if modules are to be ready on time and are to be linked into a working program and the whole delivered on schedule, system designers and programmers must be subject to a working discipline. Schedules must be closely controlled, and the system-program configuration must be tightly managed. The aforesaid is the job of the configuration control chief.

13.6. Configuration Control

The configuration control chief maintains four sets of records:

1. Schedules—bar charts and circle charts

2. Written documentation

3. The computer program library

4. Automated records of module interfaces

Maintenance of overall scheduling records—bar charts and circle charts—is the responsibility of configuration control. Written program documentation must be in a form readable by humans. Documents should be as thorough as possible and clear enough to guarantee communication among the teams that did the original design, new personnel, and those charged with postdeployment support. Documentation includes:

- Scheduling charts
- Program trees
- HIPO diagrams
- Printouts of computer programs
- Automated module interface records

Since scheduling charts and program trees have already been discussed, let us proceed to HIPO diagrams.

13.6.1. HIPO diagrams

The acronym HIPO means Hierarchy plus Input-Process-Output. The use of HIPO diagrams is a technique popularized by IBM as both a documentation methodology and an aid to support top-down structured programming. HIPO diagrams describe the functions of modules and support Ada configuration management.

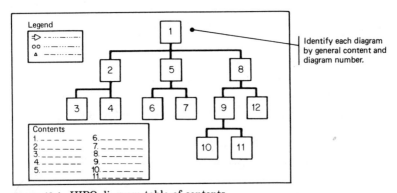

Figure 13.4 HIPO diagram table of contents.

HIPO diagrams are organized into packets, each consisting of sets of operational diagrams that describe system functions from the general to the detail level. Typically, a HIPO packet consists of a visual table of contents as shown in Figure 13.4, overview diagrams as shown in Figure 13.5, and detail diagrams as shown in Figure 13.6.

The table of contents page shows a legend, a program tree that identifies the detailed diagrams that follow, and a summary of the overall packet contents. With this introductory page, the reader can locate a particular level of information or a specific diagram without thumbing through the entire package.

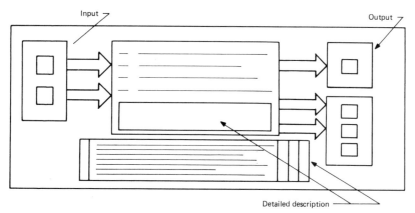

Figure 13.5 HIPO diagram, module overview.

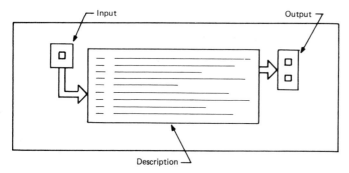

Figure 13.6 HIPO diagram, detailed description of module.

The overview detail diagrams describe each function of the module. The individual diagrams show:

- The process that supports the function described
- Results of the process
- Necessary inputs
- Resulting outputs

The number of levels of detailed diagrams is determined by the number of functional subprograms that comprise the module and the complexity of the material.

HIPO diagrams are helpful to people who rely on documentation for many different purposes. For example:

- The project manager may want to keep an overview of the system on his desk.
- Programmers need the documentation to determine the detailed operation of modules that are to be programmed.
- In postdeployment support, programmers require documentation that quickly identifies modules in which changes are made.
- New personnel will need the diagrams to learn the system.

HIPO diagrams meet needs such as the above because they are graphical representations of each module.

In summary, HIPO diagrams provide aid and improvement in:

- Systematic identification of project requirements
- The definition of programming tasks
- Defining functional interfaces
- Providing smooth information transfer among personnel
- Documentation methodologies
- Planning system testing
- Achieving quick retrieval of information and faster fixes in the postdeployment support environment

13.6.2. The Program Library

From time to time throughout this text we have referred to the program library. By definition, the *program library* is a collection of compilation units—both predefined and programmer defined—resident in the host computer and controlled by the Ada programming support environment (APSE). The concept of the APSE is explained in detail in Chapter 14. For practical purposes, we may regard the program library as a collection of program units resident in the data base that is physically resident in the host computer. The program library is not resident in target computers. Recall, as explained in Section 12.0, that programs are constructed in the host computer, then transferred to the target computer.

13.6.2.1. How the program library is used. As we already know, an Ada program is comprised of library compilation units and programmer-developed units. The actual compilation process follows the pattern shown in Figure 13.7. In this sketch box 1 represents the library file of compilation units predefined in the Ada language. Box 2 represents library compilation units that were progammer-defined in a previous compilation and placed in the program library. Box 3 is the programmer-prepared program unit for this compilation. Box 4 represents new compilation units placed in the library as a result of this compilation. Box 5 is the compiled user program resulting from this compilation.

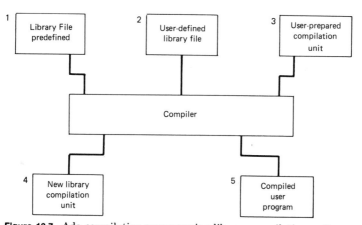

Figure 13.7 Ada compilation process using library compilation units.

13.6.3. Predefined Entities in the Program Library

Following are the principal predefined packages included in the program library and supplied with the Ada compiler.

1. CALENDAR — Provides for keeping time and dates.
2. IO_EXCEPTIONS — Defines exceptions required by the IO packages.
3. LOW_LEVEL_IO — Provides for direct control of peripheral devices.
4. SEQUENTIAL_IO and DIRECT_IO — Input-output operations for files containing elements of a single type.
5. SHARED_VARIABLE_SYNCHRONIZE — Used when two tasks share or update a variable.
6. SYSTEM — Relates to parameters of the individual computer system.
7. TEXT_IO — Applicable to text input-output readable by humans.
8. STANDARD — Provides all predefined objects and operations.

Details on the predefined packages are found in the *Reference Manual for the Ada Programming Language* identified in Section 1.11 of this book.

13.6.3.1. Automated records of module interfaces. Software support tools provided by the APSE automatically provide records of module interfaces. This means that programmers working on any given module can automatically obtain from their video screens up-to-date interface data for all modules with which they must interoperate.

13.6.4. Summary of Configuration Control

In summary, the function of configuration control is to maintain:

1. Discipline and keep the overall project on schedule
2. Written records and the Ada program library
3. Automated records provided by the APSE

13.7. System Test

Ada programmers working under the discipline of top-down structured techniques are expected to design, code, and test program modules assigned to them. But in keeping with universally accepted quality control methodology, final tests must be done by disinterested personnel not in the system and program design branch. That is the function of the system test branch shown in Figure 13.1.
System-test should follow this procedure.

1. Upon finishing the design, coding, and test of a module, the programmer forwards it to the system test organization.
2. System test:
   a. Reviews the written documentation for the module.
   b. Runs tests on the module.

If system-test determines the written documentation to be correct and complete, and if the module performs satisfactorily under test, the module is then considered complete, tested, and ready for delivery. The above discussion explains how to test individual Ada program modules. The same approach is used for overall system tests.

13.8. How the Ada Project Manager Maintains Control

To maintain control of a project, managers must know what is happening in their organizations. Managers regularly meet with their immediate lieutenants, receive reports, etc. Nevertheless, managers frequently have only a surface knowledge of what is really happening. Experience shows that the manager of a large computer programming project who does not have detailed knowledge of what is happening will run into serious delays and large cost overruns. In the experience of the author, the best tool for letting a manager know what is really happening is the structured walk-through.

13.8.1. The Structured Walk-Through

The structured walk-through is the generic term for a management tool that comprises a series of project reviews on all organizational

levels. The structured walk-through is a technique for design reviews. It may be beneficially used for managing projects that are:

- Exclusively software
- Exclusively hardware
- A combination of hardware and software

Figure 13.8—a repeat of Figure 13.3—illustrates the concept. As
previously explained, each circle in the drawing represents a module
of a hypothetical project. A program tree is associated with each
module as shown by the example of module 4. HIPO diagrams and
bar charts are also associated with module 4 and each of the other
modules.

A programming team is responsible for each module of Figure
13.8. The teams are brought together by the walk-through. Taking
module 4 as an example, the following discussion shows how the
structured walk-through works.

1. The team leader responsible for module 4 periodically calls project review meetings to which are invited representatives of everyone concerned with the project.

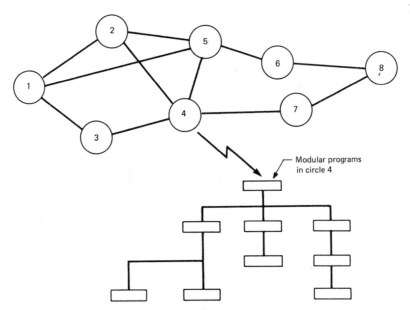

Figure 13.8 The structured walk-through.

2. In the review meeting, the team leader reports to fellow workers the progress to date on module 4. Using the program tree and starting at the top, he or she leads, or walks, attendees through the module. In addition to the circle chart, the team leader makes use of bar charts and HIPO diagrams.

Walk-throughs provide team leaders opportunities to:

- Tell other management representatives what input is needed from their teams and when it is needed.
- Highlight specific problems or successes.
- Bring future requirements or potential problems to the attention of management.

Participation in walk-throughs is of value to attendees because:

- They learn what is expected from their teams and when it is required.
- They learn how the work on the module being reported—module 4 in the example—may impact their efforts.

The structured walk-through brings together the designers and programmers for the various modules. It stimulates discussions that frequently result in improvements in the overall system design. Errors in the specifications of the individual modules are frequently discovered. In summary, experience with structured walk-throughs shows that:

1. The review is a learning experience for all attendees.
2. Project teams receive strong motivation.
3. The review is a tool for analyzing the functional design of a system, and as a result:
   a. Logical errors in program design are uncovered as a result of the analysis of the functional design.
   b. Coding errors may be eliminated before they enter the system.
4. The review is an effective management tool for determining the status of a project, managing it, and controlling it.
5. It is a framework for developing test strategies for both individual modules and overall system tests.

13.9. Personnel Relations

In the final analysis, the success of an Ada programming project depends on the interest, motivation, enthusiasm, and loyalty of employees. To develop these traits, to develop an esprit de corps within the organization, the manager must command the respect of both users and employees. As stated in the first section of this chapter, the manager is like a good football coach who has self-confidence and who demonstrates that confidence by showing confidence in team members. In showing that confidence, the coach recognizes that his football team, which is comprised of many talented players, will never be effective if he attempts to play every position for every player during the game. In other words, the coach is not on the field during the game, only on the sidelines.

To command the respect of a football team—a programming team—the Ada programming manager:

- Must understand the technical problems of engineers, system designers, and programmers and must be competent as an engineer and programmer.
- Recognizes that her or his employees are well-educated professional individuals, and demonstrates that respect for their abilities by delegating management decisions to them.
- If a particular employee shows exceptional, perhaps unrecognized abilities, he does not attempt to put that employee down, to put her in her place. Such action suggests that the manager is inherently weak and afraid the employee will get his job.
- Shows respect for the ability of employees and never talks down to them.
- Delegates management decisions to employees.
- Expects, even requires that players on the team do more than they are accustomed to doing. The manager makes employees stretch themselves to the job rather than contracting the job to fit the perceived limitations of the employee.
- Praises employees both as a team and individually for jobs well done.
- Is personally accessible to employees.
- Supports employees in handling the commonplace day-to-day problems of the business and professional worlds, i.e., supports

good working conditions, adequate pay, medical plans, vacations, etc.

13.10. What to Expect from Programmers

The synergy resulting from a combination of the Ada programming language, the discipline of top-down structured programming, and the management techniques already presented produces an efficient programming environment. Reasonable management questions are:

- What production should the Ada programming manager expect from the programming team?
- How many programmers are required?

Obviously, exact answers depend on the complexity of the programming project, but reasonably good estimates can be made by knowledgeable technical managers when the project is in the planning stage.

Generally speaking, the design, programming, and unit test of an Ada module can be handled by one programmer. Reasonably, the programmer should be expected to design, program, and test approximately fifty lines of code per day, in other words, perhaps one module per day. Overall system test—the linking and integration of modules—is easily handled by one system programmer. In the postdeployment support phase, one programmer can usually handle about 15,000 lines of program code.

Chapter

14

Compilers and the Ada Programming Support Environment

14.0. Definition of the Expression: Programming Support Environment

In broad terms, the expression *programming support environment* refers to the general domain in which computer software is designed, coded, tested, executed, and maintained. It includes compilers and all support software. In other words, it is the environment in which the programmer works.

14.1. Background

In the early days of high-level languages—essentially the period of first and second generation hardware—computers ran one program at a time; the support environment was a compiler. To use a language, a programmer wrote a program, punched it into cards, read the cards into the computer, then attempted to compile and run the program. If there were no errors, the program executed.

With the introduction of third generation hardware, computers and programs became more complex; operational features such as multiprogramming, time-sharing, remote job entry, background and foreground programs executing simultaneously, real-time operations, and the like, all became commonplace. The need for specialized software—independent program entities—to organize computer operations and to assist in the development, test, running, and postdeployment support of application programs became obvious. This software usually consisted of linkers, editors, loaders, debuggers, and utility routines.

As a general rule, support software was not planned by language designers. Commonly, development was left to individual programmers who designed special software routines for specific computers as a result of operational needs. The routines were often developed on a catch-as-catch-can basis long after the language was in use. Predictably, the results were not always good. But the more successful support programs were passed about amongst users and sometimes became industry standards.

The practice of individuals developing software support for their own needs led to duplications of effort. Frequently, individual programmers wasted time, energy, and money in developing support software that had already been developed by someone else. In essence, programmers often "reinvented the wheel." It also led to programs that operated on only one computer and programmers that were able to program only one computer.

In addition, the practice led to confused operating environments; i.e., a given computer in one installation might have one set of software support routines for a particular language, say Fortran, and in another installation, the same computer using the same Fortran compiler might have different support routines. This meant that a program written in Fortran on the first computer could not run on the same computer in the second installation.

In today's state of the art, a good many software support routines are still primarily ad hoc in nature; they are often independently developed for particular operating systems or specific hardware. This leads to dependence on one source of hardware, one operating system, and programs that cannot easily be moved from one computer to another without extensive modification. This in turn leads to programming errors, long delays, and high costs.

Early in the development of the Ada language, the Department of Defense recognized the need for support software. In setting up the High Order Language Working Group (HOLWG) in 1975, DOD's stated objective for the group was: "To produce a minimal number of common, modern high order computer languages for the DOD embedded computer systems applications and to assure a unified, well supported, widely available, and powerful programming support environment for these languages."

In short, DOD acknowledged that if we recognize the need for integrated support software in a defined programming environment in the early stages of a new language, a better-designed, more error-free universal language system results.

The DOD approach to an integrated programming support environment calls for a computer-independent user interface to the host computer operating system—if there is one—with a set of coordinated tools that will support the software system throughout its life cycle.

The DOD approach has evolved into the concept of the Ada programming support environment, known by the acronym APSE. The approach has also led to the expression, the Ada Language System; in this context, the term system is understood to include a complete set of software support tools in addition to the compiler, in short, the APSE. The expression the Ada Language System is, by definition and in broad terms, a generic term for a programming environment for use by software development teams in the production of Ada software. In a very specific sense, ALS is the Army implementation of the Ada language program.

14.2. Description of the APSE

The Ada programming support environment is detailed in a February 1980 DOD publication called the *Stoneman*. An APSE specification derived from the *Stoneman* has not been published nor is one included in the standard *Reference Manual for the Ada Programming Language*. APSE will be defined in a future standard. The *Stoneman* remains the fundamental APSE guideline.

The APSE as now conceived is hardware independent. It is a complete operationally integrated Ada programming environment that will support software systems throughout their life cycle, which encompasses conception, design, coding, testing, operational use, and modification as user requirements change. Support software entities are called software tools, support tools, or simply tools.

As stated in the above paragraph, the APSE is considered hardware independent; it can be moved from one host computer to another. To the programmer, this means the environment in which she works on computer A will be identical to the environment in which she works on computer B even though the two computers might be supplied by different manufacturers. As a result, a programmer who has been trained on a given computer can be transferred to a different computer and immediately become productive without costly retraining.

Computers manufactured by different manufacturers are never identical; no two operating systems are the same. This leads to a problem. We noted elsewhere in this book that the Ada Language System is to be deployed on any number of different host computers, and further, that operational programs will be deployed on both host and target computers. In this chapter we have also noted that to the programmer, the environment in which he works is expected to be the same regardless of which host he is using. In other words, the APSE must be common to all host computers.

From an operational standpoint, all this is impossible because the computers are not all identical. To provide an APSE common to all host computers in the environments described above, the Ada designers utilized the principles of top-down structured programming and conceived the APSE as comprising operationally independent levels. The lowest level is called the *kernel;* it is the APSE interface to the host computer system. The next level comprises an integrated set of software tools. It is frequently called the Minimum Ada Programming Support Environment (MAPSE) and includes the compiler.

Figure 14.1 illustrates the multilevel principle and the APSE interface to the host computer.

As already explained, the kernel is the section of the APSE that interfaces with the host computer operating system. Frequently it is known as the KAPSE, an acronym for Kernel Ada Programming Support Environment. The kernel is unique to each host. It is not transportable. The kernel provides the minimum set of functions necessary to interface the host and the balance of the APSE. To put it another way, linkages between the kernel and the underlying operating system are the only direct interfaces between the APSE and the host computer. The host interface with which the kernel interoperates is the Nebula Instruction Set Architecture (ISA), defined by MIL-STD 1862B, January 1983. The Ada Language System data base, including the library, is stored in the host computer system. The kernel provides the interface with the data base.

In Figure 14.1, the host operating system is designated as a modi-

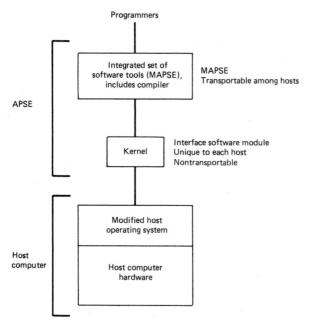

Figure 14.1   APSE host computer relationship.

fied operating system. This is because a number of the routines normally found in commonplace operating systems either are not required by Ada, or they are standardized and provided by the APSE.

The upper level of the APSE—the integrated set of software tools called the MAPSE in Figure 14.1— is universal, i.e., the same tool set is used with all host computers. It is transportable among hosts. The KAPSE-MAPSE interface separates the transportable portions of the environmental software from the nonportable. Software on the MAPSE level can be readily and inexpensively moved from one host computer to another. That on the KAPSE level cannot; it is unique to the host.

The programmer interfaces with the MAPSE. The term MAPSE was originally used to indicate that the second level included only the minimum number of software tools necessary for successful Ada programming. As now conceived, the MAPSE includes considerably more. Figure 14.2 illustrates, showing in general terms the APSE as now envisioned by the Ada Language System designers.

For convenience, Figure 14.2 illustrates the APSE by concentric circles. The innermost circle represents the kernel; it interfaces with the host. The next pair of circles is the MAPSE. Some of the principal software tools that now comprise the MAPSE are shown. All told, a complete MAPSE numbers some seventy program units. These software tools range from language translators and debugging aids to comprehensive project management support facilities.

Note that the compiler is included in the MAPSE. In other words, the compiler is a component of the integrated Ada programming support environment. Note also that the second level circles are not closed; there is an open sector. This permits programmers to add or integrate new software tools to the APSE as required. Programmers are thus able to tailor the MAPSE to specific applications

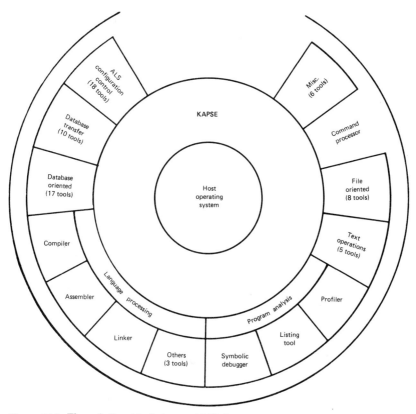

Figure 14.2 The relationship between ALS's large integrated toolset of 74 MAPSE and user-defined tools, the kernel, and the host operating system. (*SofTech, Inc.*)

without disturbing the fundamental structure of the APSE. Typical of special software entities programmers may wish to add to a given MAPSE is a simulator that represents the target computer for which they are developing a program. The APSE tools are written in Ada; software tools that are programmer-added are also written in Ada.

We have already said that the MAPSE is the portion of the APSE that may be moved from one computer to another and that the KAPSE cannot be moved. Special programmer-added tools unique to a particular installation may or may not be moved to other facilities. The APSE also permits operational programs developed on a given host and filed in the data base of that computer to be moved to another host, which may be an entirely different computer. This is called *program transportability*.

Programmers interface with the APSE on the MAPSE level; they cannot directly interface with the KAPSE. Programmers trained in the Ada Language System are really trained on the APSE. Inasmuch as the upper level of the APSE may be transported among host computers, programmers may also be shifted among hosts without extensive and costly new training. To the programmer, each APSE looks like every other APSE. The above phenomenon is called *programmer* transportability. It is important because it cuts training costs and causes programmers to work more efficiently. When programmers are moved, they do not have to spend time learning new systems; they become productive almost immediately.

14.3. What the Ada Programming Support Environment Does

The overall objective of the Department of Defense High-Order Language Program—the control and reduction of software costs throughout the software life cycle—is addressed by the design of the language and by the programming tools and libraries that make up the Ada programming support environment. We have already noted that the APSE provides a transportable programming environment and transportable programs. But to support software throughout its life cycle, much more is required. In any large programming project, at any stage in the life cycle, there are three important requirements:

1. The need for complete and accurate information on the current state of the project
2. The need for both general and special software tools
3. The need for configuration control

The data base provides a repository for accurate records of all relevant project information, all programming activities, and program libraries.

As previously noted, software tools are provided with the APSE. General tools are those that are used throughout the software life cycle. Special tools are those that are unique to certain stages of the life cycle. For example, requirements for a syntax-driven editor apply to only one stage, but requirements for a documentation system are applicable at all stages.

The need for configuration control is applicable in all life cycle stages. In the design and coding phases, effective configuration control as provided by the APSE permits teams of programmers to work independently of one another on separate modules, yet to maintain clearly defined module-to-module interfaces.

In postdeployment support, configuration control is particularly effective. As an illustration, suppose a report of an error in a target program is received. By using configuration control tools, the source text of any component of the program can be located. The actual data base objects used to generate the target program will be found, and the appropriate documentation and test histories can be located.

Once the error is traced to a specific library package and corrected, another configuration control tool is used to reconstruct the target problem and insure that the only change to the target occurs in the corrected package. Other tools enable all other programs that used the same erroneous library package to be traced and corrected.

14.4. The User Interface to the APSE

The Ada Language System is an interactive programming environment. Programmers log into the ALS at the time they sit down at their terminals. They interoperate with the command language and through that language interactively invoke the tools provided in the environment.

14.5. Importance of the Ada Programming Support Environment (APSE)

The APSE is important to the user because it:

1. Improves programmer productivity; in developing new programs, programmers save time by:
   a. Utilizing the program design features of the Ada Language System
   b. Implementing modular top-down structured design techniques
   c. Utilizing existing library compilation units

2. Improves program transportability; programs execute on different computers without modification

3. Improves programmer transportability; programmers trained on one computer do not have to undergo extensive retraining to use another computer

4. Reduces programming errors; a top-down structured approach to system design, the use of Ada as a program design language, and the firm configuration control provided by the APSE, all contribute to reducing programming errors

5. Aids both management and programmers by providing a number of capabilities to support project coordination and management

In summary, the APSE reduces the time required to develop, code, test, document, and maintain computer programs. It improves program and programmer transportability. It simplifies project coordination and assists management.

All of the above impacts costs; therefore, the APSE is a major contributor to reducing substantially the cost of programming. In light of the above, it should be noted that if an Ada compiler is provided without an integrated programming support environment, Ada is just another language, albeit a state-of-the-art language. But with the compiler embedded in the APSE, Ada is an integrated workshop for the production and maintenance of computer systems.

14.6. Status of Ada Compilers and the Overall APSE

As of the first of the year 1984, over thirty-four separate compiler and complete language system developments were in process in the United States, the United Kingdom, Finland, Denmark, Ger-

Table 14.1   Principal Department of Defense Programs

Contractor	Contract agency	Scope	Host	Target	Availability
SofTech	Army CECOM	Comprehensive APSE with *Stoneman* including production ANSI Ada compiler	VAX/VMS	Same	October 1984
Intermetrics	USAF RADC	Full Ada Language System including "Stoneman"	IBM 370	Same	Late 1984

many, France, and Japan. Through the Army, Navy, and Air Force, the Department of Defense has let contracts for the complete Ada Language System. As of the date of this writing—early spring 1984—none of the contracts is complete. The contracts are written for different host computers and different target computers. Table 14.1 outlines major DOD programs.

SofTech is also the developer for the Navy version of the Ada Language System. The Navy calls it ALS/N. It is identical to the Army system. The Air Force calls its version the Ada Integrated Environment (AIE).

A number of Ada compilers are now on the market. Table 14.2 lists the ones that have been validated by the Ada Program Office.

Other Ada compilers available as of this date are:

- Subsystems of the overall Ada Language System

- Specialized educational systems developed for training

- Versions of the ALS based on early editions of the Ada standard

Table 14.2   Certified Ada Compilers

Developer	Host Computer	Target Computer
Rolm	MSE/888 Data General 32-bit ECLIPSE	MSE/888 MSE/14 1666B

14.7. How To Acquire the Ada
Language System

Users may buy Ada compilers on the commercial market directly
from the developers. Obviously, the buyer should determine how
much of the complete Ada Language System he is actually buying.
As previously noted, many of the advertised Ada compilers are subsets of the complete Ada Language System.

14.7.1. What the Alert Company Does

In Section 14.2 of this chapter, we explained that the APSE is divided into two principal parts, the KAPSE and the MAPSE. We
pointed out that the KAPSE, or kernel, is unique to each computer
system, but that the MAPSE is transportable among computer systems. Therefore, the company that wishes to acquire the Ada Language System for its computer will not go out and buy a complete
APSE. Instead, the company will buy or acquire from the Department of Defense (see Section 14.7.2 below) only the MAPSE. It will
design the kernel to fit its own computer system.

14.7.2. The Role of the Department
of Defense

The Department of Defense is implementing use of the Ada Language System. The DOD recognizes, as pointed out in the introductory chapter of this book, that the ALS is developed with public
funds, that it is public property, and that the public must have
access. How this is accomplished, and how users may obtain the
language system through DOD sources, is discussed in Chapter 15.

15

Department of Defense
Implementation
of the Ada Language System

15.0. Basic Approach

As we have said in previous pages, the Department of Defense now requires the use of the Ada Language System in embedded computers used in tactical military systems. The basic guidance is given in DOD Directive 5000.31 which states:

> The Ada programming language shall become the single, common, computer programming language for Defense mission-critical applications. Effective January 1, 1984, for programs entering Advanced Development and July 1, 1984, for programs entering Full-Scale Engineering Development, Ada shall be the programming language. Only compilers which have been validated by the Ada Joint Program Office shall be used for software to be delivered to or maintained by the Government.

This information is consistent with a June 10, 1984, memorandum from the under secretary of defense for research and engineering to the various agencies of the DOD—called components in the memo—which states, "Ada is approved for use consistent with the introduction plans of the individual components and the validation requirements of the Ada Joint Program Office."

Each of the three armed services has its own set of draft policies and procedures for implementing regulation 5000.31. We say "draft policies and procedures" because at this early stage of the Ada program all policies and procedures are in a state of flux.

15.1. Fundamental Problem

As of the date of this book, the fundamental problem facing the services is that validated compilers for most of the computers used in embedded tactical applications are not yet available. Software support tools for the APSE are not available. General availability is not anticipated before late 1984 or 1985.

Nevertheless, the Army, Air Force, and Navy are making plans for implementing Ada, and in some cases, it is already used.

15.2. Ada as a Program Design Language

In the procurement of major military systems, each of the services is now including in requests for proposal (RFPs) statements which require contractors to use Ada as a program design language. The Army has adopted this practice as a general policy. The Navy and Air Force are permitting individual program managers to decide whether or not Ada will be used as a program design language.

The problem facing both the services and contractors is that as of the date of publication of this book, DOD has not determined which features of Ada constitute a program design language. As a result, a number of Ada-based program design languages (APDL) are in use today. These APDLs are essentially subsets of the full Ada Language System.

In responding to requests for proposal, contractors are expected to select the APDL they will use, to define it to the military program manager, and to explain how it will be used—in essence, to sell it. This means that the contractor can either use an existing APDL available from software vendors or postulate his or her own design language implementing it with selected features of the complete Ada as defined in the reference manual.

15.2.1. Army Implementation of the ALS

Consistent with DOD direction, the long-term plan of the Army is to require the use of the full Ada Language System in all acquisition programs. As pointed out in the previous chapter, current Army contracts call for the Ada Language System to be hosted on the VAX/VMS computers, targeted to the same computers, and also targeted to the military computer family (MCF). The MCF is not yet in manufacture. This spotlights two problems:

1. Inasmuch as an Army-funded ALS is not yet validated and operational, contractors may wish to use other validated compilers and support software.

2. Inasmuch as the MCF is not available, contractors may opt to rehost the ALS on other computers; or they may wish to retarget the application programs to other computers.

Both of the above actions are permissible subject to approval of the program officer.

15.2.2. Navy Implementation of the ALS

Compilers designed to be hosted on standard Navy computers are under contract. Once these compilers are available and validated, the Navy will require that new embedded computer systems be programmed in Ada. Essentially, the Navy Ada Language System is the same as that of the Army. It does, however, include special software support tools unique to Navy requirements. The Navy calls the language ALS/N.

Until Navy-contracted compilers are available, the Navy will permit the use of validated commercially developed compilers. This policy is implemented on an individual basis, i.e., permission of the program officer is required. Contractors may wish to use computers that are not standard Navy computers as either hosts or target systems. This is permissible providing approval of the program officer is obtained. Fully validated Navy compilers will be available in the 1985-1986 period.

15.2.3. Air Force Implementation of the ALS

Compilers and the complete language system for use with Air Force systems are also under contract. At this point, it does not appear that compilers will be available before early 1985, perhaps early 1985. Nevertheless, the Air Force anticipates implementing the ALS in 1984. This will be done in selected programs under controlled conditions carefully monitored by the program manager. The Air Force allows individual program managers to use commercially funded compilers pending availability of Air Force–funded compilers.

15.3. Ada Compiler Validation

The Ada Joint Program Office manages the validation of compilers. The actual validation is accomplished at designated centers. Validation centers will validate compilers developed with private funds or paid for by DOD contract. In the event of a work overload at a validation center, DOD-funded compilers will be given priority. Validation is based on the Ada standard, ANSI/MIL-STD 1815A, January 1983.

As of the date of this writing, validation centers are still being selected. The initial centers are located as follows:

> Army: Headquarters
>   Communications-Electronics Command
>   Fort Monmouth, NJ 07703

> Air Force: Commanding Officer
>   Rome Air Development Center
>   Rome, NY 13440

The Institute for Defense Analysis in Arlington, Virginia is delegated overall responsibility for coordinating validation. In addition, the General Services Administration is considering the establishment of an Ada validation center. Establishment of validation centers in West Germany, France, and the United Kingdom is under consideration. Schedules for establishing the additional centers are uncertain.

All validation centers will use the same tests, and they will operate under the same guidelines. All certificates will be equally valid. Validation tests will be conducted for every possible combination of host computer, target computer, and run-time environment. Ada Joint Program Office procedures require that contractors submit compilers for revalidation on an annual basis. If a compiler fails to pass its annual test, validation will be withdrawn. When implementing Ada, contractors will be expected to use the latest version of a validated compiler.

15.4. Distribution of the ALS

Under the cognizance of the Ada Joint Program Office, each of the three military services is establishing its own policies regarding distribution of the ALS to contractors. Procedural details are still in the planning stage, but generally speaking, each service will provide the ALS to contractors as government-furnished property (GFP); this means on loan at no cost to the contractor.

As pointed out in Chapter 14, which explained the Ada programming support environment (APSE), the MAPSE section of the APSE provides for incorporating programmer-developed software tools should such be required for a specific installation. These tools are not part of the standard MAPSE; they are considered optional. Some of the optional tools may be developed with DOD money. In this event, the tool is government property; it may be made available to contractors as GFP at the discretion of the program manager.

The services will provide maintenance support for components of the ALS loaned to contractors as GFP. Should contractors acquire the ALS, even a validated ALS, from a software vendor, maintenance support will not be provided by the government. In other words, the contractor and the vendor must make separate support arrangements.

15.5. Nonmilitary Use of the ALS

Department of Defense policies and procedures relating to distributing the DOD-funded ALS to colleges and universities for study and training or to industry for commercial use are under study. As of this date, no specific policies or procedures have been announced.

15.6. The Ada Information Clearinghouse

To facilitate distribution of information on the Ada language to the user community and the general public, the Ada Joint Program Office has established the Ada Information Clearinghouse. The address is:

Ada IC
3D139(400AN)
The Pentagon
Washington, D.C. 20301

Appendix A

Predefined Language Environment

The definition of the Ada Language System includes the following predefined library units:

- package CALENDAR
- generic procedure UNCHECKED_DEALLOCATION
- generic function UNCHECKED_CONVERSION
- generic package SEQUENTIAL_IO
- generic package DIRECT_IO
- package TEXT_IO
- package IO_EXCEPTIONS
- package LOW_LEVEL_IO
- package SYSTEM
- package STANDARD

With the exception of STANDARD, use of the above packages, procedure, and function is discussed at appropriate points in the text. Details on the contents are provided in the *Reference Manual For the Ada Programming Language*.

The predefined package STANDARD contains all predefined identifiers in the Ada language. When programming in Ada, it not necessary to specify STANDARD in the program entity on which we are working. The package is automatically instantiated when a library unit is translated. What happens is this: When a library unit is translated, the compiler treats the unit as if it were declared at the end of the specification of STANDARD. This makes all predefined identifiers automatically available and directly visible.

Glossary

Accept statement: See entry statement.

Assignment: The operation that replaces the current value of a variable by a new value.

Body: The action part of an Ada program entity. It comprises the sequence of statements that perform the functions of the program unit. Program units are subprograms, packages, or tasks.

Compilation unit: An Ada program entity; it may be called a module. It may contain a declaration, a body, or both a declaration and a body. It is compiled as a separate entity.

Declarative part: The section of a program entity that defines the program units used in the entity. It is also known as the *specification*.

Elaboration: The process by which the declaration achieves its effect, for example, creating an object. The process occurs during program execution.

Entry statement: The means by which communication between tasks is accomplished. Externally, an entry is called in the same way a subprogram is called. Its internal behavior is specified by one or more accept statements specifying the actions to be performed when the entry is called.

Exception: An error situation which may arise during program execution. To raise an exception is to stop program execution so as to signal that an error has occurred. An exception handler is a software routine that specifies a response to the exception. Execution of the exception handler is called handling the exception.

Expression: The basis by which the computation of a value is defined.

Function: See *subprogram*.

Generic unit: A template either for a set of subprograms or for a set of packages. A subprogram or package created using the template is called an instance of the generic unit. A generic instantiation is the declaration that creates an instance. A generic unit is written as a subprogram or a package but with the specification prefixed by a generic formal part which may declare generic formal parameters. A generic formal parameter is a type, a subprogram, or an object.

Handler: See *exception.*

Identifier: A basic lexical element of the language used as the name of an entity.

Module: An Ada program entity, i.e., subprogram, package, task, and/or generic unit.

Object: A value which may be a variable or a constant. A program creates an object by elaborating an object declaration.

Overloading: The property of an identifier having several alternative meanings at a given point in a program text. The effective meaning of an overloaded identifier is determined by the context.

Package: One of the program units or modules from which overall programs are constructed. It is a collection of logically related program entities grouped or packaged together. Packages provide the means for treating a collection of program entities as a single unit. They generally comprise two separate parts: the specification and the body, or action part. The specification and the body may reside in separate library files. They may be compiled separately and at different times. The package body is not visible to users; only the specification is visible. The package specification may include a private part. This is a section that contains structural details that are irrelevant to the user but complete the specification of the visible entities. The private part is not visible to users.

Pragma: An instruction to the compiler; it conveys information to the compiler and, in a sense, permits the programmer to talk to the compiler. In so doing, it causes the compiler to perform programmer-directed operations.

Private part: That part of the package specification that contains structural information completing the specification, the details of which are hidden from users, i.e., not visible because they are irrelevant to the user. See also *package.*

Private type: A type whose structure and set of values are clearly defined but not directly available or known to the user. It is known by its discriminates and the set of operations defined for it. The private type and its applicable operations are defined in the visible part of the specification.

Program: In Ada, one that comprises a number of compilation units, one of which is a subprogram called the main program. Execution of the program consists of executing the main program, which may invoke subprograms declared in the other compilation units.

Program unit: Any of the following: generic unit, package, subprogram, or task.

Raising an exception: See *exception.*

Rendezvous: The interaction that occurs between two tasks executing in parallel when one task calls an entry of the other task and a corresponding accept statement is executed by the called task on behalf of the calling task.

Specification: See *declarative part.*

Subprogram: An Ada program unit that is either a procedure or a function. A procedure specifies a sequence of actions and it is invoked by a procedure call. A function specifies a sequence of actions and returns a result. A function call is an expression. A subprogram comprises two parts, a declaration and a body. The declaration specifies the name of the subprogram and its parameters. The body specifies its execution.

Tasks: Program entities that may execute in parallel. In other words, tasks provide the facilities for parallel execution of subprocesses of a main program module. Tasks may execute on multicomputer configurations, or they may interleave on a single computer. Tasks are not independent program units. They are nested entities and operate within an Ada program module, i.e., a procedure or a package. Tasks comprise a specification and a body. The declaration specifies the name of the task and its parameters; the body specifies its execution.

Type: A specification of both a set of values and a set of operations applicable to those values. Identifiers and variables are typed.

Index

accept statement, 29, 42
Access:
  direct, 61–62, 65–67
  sequential, 61–62, 65
Access types, 20
Action part, 11, 35, 48, 142
Ada, 79–80
  background of, 3
  benefits due to use of, 2
  defined, 1
  impact of, 2–3
  implementation of, 5
  market for, 2
  requirement for, 2
  standards for, 5
  as system-program design language,
    85–87
  (*See also* Language *entries*)
Ada-based program design languages
  (APDL), 136
Ada compilers, 132–133
Ada Integrated Environment (AIE), 133
Ada Joint Program Office, 138
Ada Language System (ALS), 1, 4, 7, 126
  acquiring, 134
  Air Force implementation of, 133, 137
  Army implementation of, 133, 136–137
  defined, 140–141
  distribution of, 138–139
  DOD implementation of, 135–139
  Navy implementation of, 133, 137
  Navy version of (ALS/N), 133, 137
  nonmilitary use of, 139
Ada programming support environment
  (APSE), 4, 126–134
  description of, 126–130
  function of, 130–131
  importance of, 132
  status of overall, 132
  user interface to, 131
Addition, 13

AIE (Ada Integrated Environment), 133
Air Force implementation of ALS, 133,
  137
Algorithms, 90
ALS (*see* Ada Language System)
APDL (Ada-based program design
  languages), 136
Application programming, 85, 100
APSE (*see* Ada programming support
  environment)
Army implementation of ALS, 133, 136–
  137
Array notation, 32
Array operations, 32–33
Array specification, 31
Arrays, 19–20, 31–34
  constrained, 19
  defined, 31
  one-dimensional, 31
  two-dimensional, 31, 32
  unconstrained, 20
ASCII characters, 17–18
Assignment, 142
Assignment statement, 12
Asterisks, 14
Automated records of module interfaces,
  118

Bar charts, 111–112
begin, 35
Blanks, 12
Body, 11, 35, 48, 142
  package, 48, 50
Boolean types, 18–19
Brackets, double, 28, 29

CALENDAR, 118, 140
Call statements, 29
Called tasks, 43
Calling tasks, 43

case statement, 25
CHARACTER, 17–18
Character set, 11
Characters, 67
  ASCII, 17–18
  input-output of, 70–71
Charts:
  bar, 111–112
  circle, 112–113
Circle charts, 112–113
Circuit concepts, 95–96
Circular networks, 94
CLOSE procedure, 63
Closed files, 62
Closing files, 63
COL function, 70
Columns, 67
Commas, 34
Comments, 13
Communication system, 95–96
Compilation process, 117
Compilation units, 83, 142
Compiler validation, 138
Compilers, 4, 124
  Ada, 132–133
Composite types, 19–20
Computer software, 82–83
Computers:
  embedded, 81, 82
  host, 81, 82
  target, 81, 82
Conditional control structures, 23–26
Conditional **select,** 46
Configuration control, 113–118, 131
Constrained arrays, 19
CONSTRAINT ERROR, 59
Control statements, 27–30
  nested, 28
Control structures, 23–26
CONTROLLED, 56
CREATE procedure, 63
Current index, 62
Current size, 62

Data, 16–22
  defined, 16
Data elements, 32
Data object, 19
Declarations, 14
Declarative part, 142
Decomposition procedure, 89
Delay, **select,** 47

DELETE procedure, 64
Department of Defense (DOD), 2–6, 125–126, 133, 134
  implementation of ALS, 135–139
Design languages, 85
Direct access, 61–62, 65–67
Direct files, 62, 63
Direct input-output, 65–67
DIRECT_IO, 61, 62, 118, 140
Division, 13, 14
do-until statement, 91
Documentation, 114
DOD (*see* Department of Defense)
Dynamic testing, 106

either-or statement, 90
ELABORATE, 56
Elaboration, 142
else condition, 24
elsif condition, 23–24
Embedded computers, 81, 82
end if, 24
END_OF_FILE function, 65
END_OF_FILE test, 69–70
END_OF_LINE test, 69
END_OF_PAGE functions, 69
entry statement, 42, 142
Enumeration types, 17–18
Errors, 58
Exception handlers, 58, 59
Exceptions, 14, 26, 58–60, 142
  examples of, 60
  handling, 58, 59
  predefined, 59
  raising, 58
  user-defined, 59
exit statement, 27–28
Exponentiation, 13, 14
Exponents, 14
Expressions, 14, 142
External files, 62, 63

Fan-in operation, 95
File management, 63–65
File modes, 62–63
Files, 61, 62
  closed, 62
  closing, 63
  direct, 62, 63
  external, 62, 63
  internal, 62
  open, 62
  opening, 63

Files (*Cont.*):
  sequential, 62, 63
Fixed point numbers, 18
Floating point numbers, 18
for statement, 26–27
Format, structured programming, 14
FROM parameter, 66
Function call, 29
Functions, 10, 35, 37–38

Generic instantiation, 74, 76
Generics, 15, 74–78, 87, 142–143
  creating, 74–75
  example of, 76–77
  general, 74
  instances of, 76
  instantiating, 74, 76
  summary considerations for, 77–78
GET procedure, 67, 70, 71
GFP (government furnished property),
  138–139
Glossary, 142–144
goto statement, 28–29
Government furnished property (GFP),
  138–139
Graphics technique, stylized, 101–102

Handlers, exception, 58, 59
Hierarchy plus Input-Process-Output
  (HIPO) diagrams, 114–116
High Order Language Working Group
  (HOLWG), 125
HIPO (Hierarchy plus Input-Process-
  Output) diagrams, 114–116
HOLWG (High Order Language Working
  Group), 125
Host computers, 81, 82
Hyphens, two, 13, 86

Identifiers, 12, 16, 143
if statement, 23–24
Implementation-defined pragmas, 57
IN_FILE mode, 63
in out, 36
Indefinite wait, 46
Index, 31, 32
  current, 62
Index number one, 62
INLINE, 56
INOUT_FILE mode, 63
Input-output, 14, 61–73
  of characters and strings, 70–71

Input-output (*Cont.*):
  direct, 65–67
  introduction to, 61
  low-level, 71–72
  sequential, 65
  terminology for, 61–63
  text, example of, 72–73
Instances of generics, 76
Instants, 76
Integer numbers, 18
Internal files, 62
IO_EXCEPTIONS, 61, 118, 140
is, 17–18
ISA (Nebula Instruction Set
  Architecture), 127
ITEM parameter, 66

KAPSE (Kernel Ada Programming Support Environment), 127–128, 130,
  134
Kernel, 127
Kernel Ada Programming Support
  Environment (KAPSE), 127–128,
  130, 134

Labels, 28, 29
Language basics, 9–15
Language environment, predefined, 140–
  141
Language structure, 9
Library, program, 116–118
Library generic (*see* Generics)
LINE function, 70
Line length, 67–68
Line terminator, 69
LIST, 56
Logic types, 18–19
Loops, 26–27
  basic, 26
  for, 26–27
  while, 27
Low-level input-output, 71–72
LOW_LEVEL_IO, 61, 118, 140

Maintenance, system, 108–109
Management, 107–123
  defined, 107
Management psychology, 110
Managers:
  attributes of, 107–108
  maintaining control by, 119–121
  programming, 122–123

MAPSE (Minimum Ada Programming Support Environment), 127–130, 134, 139
Mathematical statements, 13–14
Matrix, 32
MCF (military computer family), 136–137
MEMORY_SIZE, 56
Message concentration, principle of, 95
Message deconcentration, principle of, 95
Military computer family (MCF), 136–137
Minimum Ada Programming Support Environment (MAPSE), 127–130, 134, 139
Modes, 62–63
Modularizing system designs, 88–91
Module interfaces, automated records of, 118
Module testing, 106
Modules, 83, 88, 91, 143
  detailed description of, 115
  linking, 91–93
  overview of, 115, 116
  relationships among, 111–113
Months of the year, 17
Multiplication, 13, 14

Navy implementation of ALS, 133, 137
Nebula Instruction Set Architecture (ISA), 127
Nesting, 101–102
  control statements, 28
  tasks, 40
NEW_LINE procedure, 68
NEW_PAGE procedure, 69
Node switches in packet networks, 96–100
  design of, 98–100
Nodes, 87
null, 24
Numbers:
  fixed point, 18
  floating point, 18
  integer, 18
  roman, 18
NUMERIC ERROR, 59
Numeric types, 18

Object declarations, 19
Objects, 143
OFF, 56

ON, 56
One-dimensional array, 31
Open files, 62
OPEN procedure, 63
Opening files, 63
Operating systems, 4
Operational situations, exceptional, 14
Operations, order of, 14
OPTIMIZE, 57
or alternatives, 45
Order of operations, 14
Organization, 108–110
others, 25–26
OUT_FILE mode, 63
Output (see Input-output)
Overloading, 18, 38–39, 143

PACK, 57
Package access, 53–54
Package body, 48, 50
Package specification, 49
Packages, 9, 10, 48–54, 143
  example, 50–52
Packet message switch, 93
Packet message systems, 93–95
Packet networks, 94–95
  node switches in, 96–100
PAGE, 57, 70
Page length, 67–68
Page terminator, 69
Parentheses, 14
Parents, 40
Personnel relations, 122–123
PERT scheduling, 113
Pop operation, 75
Postdeployment support, 108–109
Pragmas, 55–58, 143
  implementation-defined, 57
  predefined, 56–57
  special, 57–58
Precision, 18
Predefined, 22
Predefined types, 22
PRIORITY, 57
private, 52–53
Private part, 143
Private types, 20–21, 143
procedure, 50–51
Procedure call, 29
Procedures, 9–10, 35–37
Program construction, 10–11
PROGRAM ERROR, 59

Program library, 116–118
Program modules, 9
  (*See also* Modules)
Program transportability, 130
Program trees, 87, 88
  developing, 90–91
  developing system-programs designs
    using, 91
  top-down decomposition into, 103
Program units, 143
Program validation, 101–102
Programmer remarks, 13
Programmers, 123
Programming format, structured, 14
Programming managers, 122–123
Programming support environment,
  124
Programming team, 120–121
Programs, 81–106, 143
  introduction to, 81
  testing, 102–105
Push operation, 75
PUT procedure, 67, 70, 71

Quotes:
  double, 34
  single, 18

raise statement, 25–26, 60
Raising exceptions, 58
READ procedure, 65–66, 70
RECEIVE_CONTROL procedure, 71–72
Records, 20
  automated, of module interfaces, 118
*Reference Manual for the Ada
  Programming Language*, 5
Remarks, programmer, 13
Rendezvous, 41–43, 45, 144
Requests for proposal (RFPs), 136
Reserved words, 12–13
RESET procedure, 64
return statement, 29–30, 37
RFPs (requests for proposal), 136
Roman numbers, 18

Scalar types, 17
Scheduling, 113
  PERT, 113
select, conditional, 46
select delay, 47
SELECT ERROR, 59
Select statements, 45–47

select wait, 45
SEND_CONTROL procedure, 71
Sequential access, 61–62, 65
Sequential files, 62, 63
Sequential input-output, 65
SEQUENTIAL_IO, 61, 62, 118, 140
SET_COL procedure, 70
SHARED, 57
SHARED_VARIABLE_
  SYNCHRONIZE, 118
Siblings, 40
Significant figures, 18
SKIP_LINE procedure, 69
Slashes, 14
  double, 86
Software:
  computer, 82–83
  support, 125
Software testing, 105–106
Sort procedures, 35–36, 85
SPACE, 57
SPACING, 68–69
Specification part, 11, 35, 48
Stacks, 75
STANDARD, 118, 140–141
Statements, 14
  assignment, 12
  call, 29
  control, 27–30
  mathematical, 13–14
  select, 45–47
Static analysis, 105–106
STATUS_ERROR, 65
Stoneman, 126
STORAGE ERROR, 59
STORAGE_UNIT, 57
STRING, 34
Strings, 34
  input-output of, 70–71
Strong typing, 22
Structured programming, 90
  top-down (*see* Top-down structured
    programming)
Structured programming format, 14
Structured walk-through, 119–121
Stylized graphics technique, 101–102
Subprograms, 9–10, 35–39, 144
  written in other languages, 58
Subscripts, 32
Subtraction, 13
Support, postdeployment, 108–109
Support environment, programming, 124

Support software, 125
SUPPRESS, 57
Symbol ◇, 20, 36
SYSTEM, 118, 140
System design, 84–93
  example, 93–100
  modularizing, 88–91
System maintenance, 108–109
SYSTEM_NAME, 57
System-program design language, 84–85
  Ada as, 85–87
  methodology of, 87–88
System-program designs, developing, 91
System test, 106, 119
  and reliability, 100–106

Target computers, 81, 82
Task structure, 41–42
TASKING ERROR, 59
Tasks, 9, 10, 40–47, 144
  called, 43
  calling, 43
  example of, 43–45
  multiple, 10
  nesting, 40
Team leaders, 120–121
Test condition, 26
Text input-output, example of, 72–73
TEXT_IO, 61, 118, 140
TEXT_IO package, 67–70
then, 23–24
Threads, 40
TIME, 57
TO parameter, 66, 68
Top-down decomposition, 103
Top-down structured programming, 88–89
  basic rules of, 91
  developing program trees using, 90–91
Transportability, program, 130

Trees, program (see Program trees)
Two-dimensional array, 31, 32
type, 17–18
Types, 17, 144
  access, 20
  boolean, 18–19
  composite, 19–20
  enumeration, 17–18
  logic, 18–19
  numeric, 18
  predefined, 22
  private, 20–21, 143
  scalar, 17
Typing, 16–17, 21
  strong, 22

UNCHECKED_CONVERSION, 140
UNCHECKED_DEALLOCATION, 140
Unconstrained arrays, 20
Underscore symbols, 12
use clause, 53–54
User-defined exceptions, 59

Validation, 105–106
  compiler, 138
  program, 101–102
Validation centers, 138
Variables, 12

Wait:
  indefinite, 46
  select, 45
Wait state, 43
Walk-through, structured, 119–121
when choices, 25
while statement, 27
with clause, 53–54
Words, reserved, 12–13
WRITE procedure, 65, 66, 70

ABOUT THE AUTHOR

Philip I. Johnson is Chief of Technical Management and
Support at the Center for System Engineering and In-
tegration Headquarters, U.S. Army Communications-
Electronics Command, Fort Monmouth, New Jersey.
Mr. Johnson served previously as head of the Computer
Center at Illinois Institute of Technology as well as in
engineering management positions with General Elec-
tric, Hughes Aircraft, and RCA.